Cooking for Wine

ANN & TONY KISCHNER
WITH CHERI WALKER

HARRIS & FRIEDRICH
OCEAN PARK, WASHINGTON

Library of Congress Catalog Card Number: 91-73383

ISBN 1-880166-01-1

Color Photography: Joel Levin

Book Design: April Ryan

ImageSetting: Word Graphics, Inc., Redmond, WA

Printing: A Graphic Resource, St. Louis, MO

Literary Editor: Elisabeth McPherson

Culinary Editor: Margo Maier

Printed and bound in the United States of America.

DEDICATION

The restaurant game, like any other sport, can only be played consistently well (and won) through the collective efforts, strong intentions and extended tenure of its team members. In ten years we have had the good fortune to establish, maintain and constantly improve a lofty regional and national reputation. In ten years, we have also had the exceptional luck to attract and often keep a great number of talented and caring people in our employ (several have been with us since the day we opened).

We, therefore, dedicate this book to our staff, both past and present. It is clearly only due to your contribution of time, hard work, sweat, dedication and love that The Shoalwater has achieved the reputation and notice it has received. We appreciate and thank you for all you have given, and for hanging in there with us through thick and thin. The restaurant's success is—and will continue to be—your success. Please take a well-deserved bow with us!

TABLE OF CONTENTS

TABLE OF CONTENTS

TABLE OF CONTENTS

Preface

Tony and Ann Kischner named their first restaurant on the Long Beach Peninsula Shoalwater, after the shallow bay to the east that we now call, more prosaically, Willapa Harbor. The Peninsula, a ten-thousand-year-old by-blow from the continuous buffeting between the Columbia River and the Pacific Ocean, stretches due north from the river mouth for thirty miles, and is slim, like a worm; barely a mile of sandspit, overgrown with vegetation, separates sea from bay.

How this spit remains so gracefully slender is a mystery, for it is stuffed with food. Settlers in the early 1850s wrote home that when the tide was out, the table was set. Oysters spawned by the millions in the bay, as did razor clams in the Pacific breakers. Dungeness crabs choked water holes at ebb tide, and salmon and sturgeon jostled for room offshore. Inland, trout leaped at the hook, and deer and elk sought out the hunter. Wildfowl were so dense in the heavens that they kept off the endless drench of the rain.

The settlers were not always particular about what they ate. Bear would do in a pinch. They relished goose, duck, swan, and snipe, but would not turn up their noses at pelican, stork, seagull, or owl. On Christmas day, 1851, James Swan served James Purdington a meal featuring two crows. "I kin swallow *crow," remarked Captain Purdington, "but hanged if I* hanker *arter it."*

Drive ten or twelve miles north from the Shoalwater Restaurant and you will come across the remains of a village called Oysterville, where I was a squalling infant in the year 1910. By then the population of native oysters had dwindled, and the Pacific variety that now supports a thriving local industry had not yet shown up. There were surviving members of the original species still hiding away, though, in sloughs along the bay channel, and my father (who knew about such matters, having himself been born in Oysterville, to an oysterman, in 1876) could always bring home enough of them to half-fill a dripping gunnysack.

We did not delight in such delicacies every day: we saved them for company. The first course on these occasions was oyster cocktails or oysters on the half shell, followed by oyster soup and an entrée of fried oysters or oyster stew. Memory tells me that dessert consisted of oysters dunked in chocolate sauce; but my sister Dale refuses to confirm this.

A quarter of a century or so ago, tourists discovered the Peninsula, and menus became considerably more sophisticated. Today we boast a full gamut of restaurants, to some of which worshippers make pilgrimages from as far away as New York, London, or even, on a fine day, Tokyo.

None beats the Kischners' Shoalwater, located in the legendary Shelburne Inn at Seaview. When Tony says a dish is superb, you have to believe him. This book contains his own favorite recipes, and I suspect you will eat it up.

You will find no entry for roast crow.

Willard R. Espy
Oysterville 23 May 1991

Cooking for Wine

1991. *The release of this cookbook marks our tenth anniversary at the Shelburne Inn, but we really have been writing it for the entire ten years we have operated the Shoalwater Restaurant. Although it highlights a specific series of meals—the monthly wine dinners—it represents the wide variety of our constantly changing repertoire. The recipes also trace the evolution of our own version of Pacific Northwest cookery. (Notice how I try to eliminate controversy by avoiding the dangerous term "cuisine"!)*

As you use this book, don't be intimidated by its format. These fancy sounding meals are really chef-friendly. We have worked hard to insure that the composite dinners presented here work well both as complementary courses and in combination with the specific Northwest wines we have recommended. But all the recipes can be prepared individually, as we do most of the time. Or they can be combined with other dishes in other parts of the book, as simply or elaborately as you wish.

We are quite aware that not everyone today has the equipment, supplies and time—or their doctor's permission—to prepare meals like these at home. Nothing would please us more, of course, than to hear that somebody had gotten excited enough to exclaim, "Honey, let's do

Chapter Three tonight!" but we realize that can't happen all the time. Our advice is to prepare as much or as little as will work for you. And whether you're cooking for two or for twelve, remember that many of these recipes can be either appetizers or main courses; decide what you want and adjust the quantities accordingly.

Just as most of the menus presented here are more elaborate than anyone prepares regularly at home, so more wine is suggested than it is probably wise to consume at one time. For each recipe we have recommended a specific wine which we think will do it justice, but we leave it to your discretion and sense of balance—considering, of course, the number of guests you're serving—to decide how many different wines it's appropriate to open for a multi-course meal with friends. The choice can be as simple as a red and white for dinner or as complex as a progression of various whites and reds—but in that case, ask your friends for their car keys before you sit down to the table.

Our recommendations clearly leave room for interpretation and adjustment according to local availability and personal preference. Happily, the Pacific Northwest now offers an embarrassment of riches. Though the choice is not yet as overwhelming as it is in California, more than 125 wineries in this area represent the full range of fine varietal wines. Each new vintage brings continued refinement to the industry's overall quality, and the relatively new Pacific Northwest wineries are beginning to receive well deserved respect in the world wine community. That's why we have kept our focus on regional wines, leaving you to find other options if you can't find these excellent northwest wines in your local wine shop or grocery store. But in that case, please complain!

Many years before we arrived at the Shelburne, these words were carefully scripted on the ceiling beams in the original dining room: ***"EAT, DRINK AND BE MERRY — OF TOMORROW TAKE NO HEED."*** *They are still there.*

We do plan for tomorrow, but those words serve as a reminder of why we keep living the crazy lives required of restaurant people. We keep on because we want our guests to enjoy good food and drink prepared lovingly and served in a comforting environment. We want people to be merry.

We have written this cookbook in the same spirit. We hope these recipes will help you create your own love and merriment and let you forget, at least temporarily, tomorrow's cares.

COLUMBIA
CHATEAU STE. MICHELLE/
COLUMBIA CREST
CHINOOK

BLACKBERRY SCALLOP CEVICHE
Chinook Winery Washington Semillon (Topaz)

SPRING NETTLE SOUP
Columbia Winery Washington Gewürztraminer

OR

LEMON CHICKEN SOUP
Chateau Ste. Michelle Washington Johannisberg Riesling

STURGEON & MUSSELS EN COCOTTE
Columbia Crest Columbia Valley Sauvignon Blanc

OR

NORTHWEST CIOPPINO
Columbia Red Willow Vineyard (Milestone) Merlot

SHOALWATER SEAFOOD FETTUCCINE
Columbia Wykoff Vineyards Chardonnay

OR

RAVIOLI APERTO
Chinook Columbia Valley Chardonnay

GRILLED LAMB CHOPS WITH
GREEN PEPPER & HONEY MUSTARD SAUCE
Chateau Ste. Michelle Cold Creek Vineyard Cabernet Sauvignon

CHOCOLATE PEAR CAKE
Whidbey's Washington Port

OR

PUMPKIN SHERRY FLAN
Columbia Winery Cellarmaster's Reserve Johannisberg Riesling

Columbia
Chateau Ste. Michelle/
Columbia Crest
Chinook

Whenever we stop long enough to look at the forest instead of the trees, we have to admit that we have been fortunate to be in the right place at the right time throughout our restaurant careers. (Of course, how an English major raised in Brazil (Tony) and a Psychology major born in New York (Ann), hooked up with a Music major (Cheri) and an insurance agent (Cheri's husband, our manager Blaine) from Seattle to start up a restaurant on the southwest Washington coast is an interesting story in itself, but for another day.)

As it happened, the timing of our accidental start in the food service business (serving meals at our college dorms) coincided exactly with the inception of today's extensive wine industry in the Pacific Northwest. In the late 1960s, as we pursued our undergraduate degrees and tried to figure out what to do with them, three formative events occurred in the local wine world: a group of home-winemaking academics at the University of Washington legalized their expanding hobby by establishing The Associated Vintners (now Columbia Winery); the founder of Washington's American Wine Growers created Ste. Michelle Vintners (today known as Chateau Ste. Michelle) to pursue premium wine varietals; and, in Oregon, modern-day pioneer David Lett honed in on the Dundee Hills in the Willamette Valley southwest of Portland after a world-wide search to find the best location to produce fine wines from the great Burgundian varietals, Chardonnay and Pinot Noir.

As we decided to enter the restaurant field in earnest after college, we encountered a fast-changing regional food scene and began to become aware of the small but growing regional wine industry. As the manager and wine steward of Rosellini's Other Place Restaurant in Seattle, I had the opportunity to meet all the new regional winemakers as they vied for a position on that restaurant's extraordinary, award-winning wine list. I also tasted all their releases extensively, in order to provide our already sophisticated clientele with introductions to the region's new wines. Increased familiarity with the wines and personalities involved brought me to appreciate, respect and enjoy them more and more, and I began to shift my allegiance from European and California producers to those in our own back yard. This tied in very nicely with the increasing regional focus in The Other Place's kitchen. Those were the cutting edge days, and I remember them fondly. When Ann and I moved from Seattle to Seaview to open our own restaurant, we transplanted that excitement about the foods and the wines of the region and did our best to infuse it into our own place.

Blackberry Scallop Ceviche

1½ c olive oil
1 c blackberry juice
1 c orange juice
¾ c lemon juice
¾ c lime juice
1 red onion, julienned
4 shallots, minced
1 tsp garlic, minced
1 oz anise hyssop, chopped
½ tsp salt
½ tsp black pepper
½ tsp Magic Dust (or cayenne pepper)
3 lb fresh sea scallops
2 c Blackberry Marinated Onions
1 c Blackberry Ketchup, for garnish
anise hyssop or lemon, lime & orange slices, for garnish

This is one of those presentations that looks almost too good to eat. Combining with the recipes for Blackberry Ketchup and Blackberry Marinated Onions, this ceviche brings together some of the best of our regional bounty, delicate scallops and sun-ripened blackberries, for a fine blending of subtle flavor and texture.

Combine all the ingredients except the scallops, Blackberry Marinated Onions and Blackberry Ketchup. When well mixed, add the scallops and marinate refrigerated for 8 hours or overnight.

Make nests on each plate out of the Blackberry Marinated Onions. Arrange some scallops in the center and spoon the marinade over the top. Garnish with Blackberry Ketchup and fresh anise hyssop or slices of lemon, lime and orange.

Makes 6 entrée servings or 8 to 12 appetizers.

Years ago, half of the building that now comprises the Shelburne Inn was moved from across the street and joined to an existing structure to create the Inn as David Campiche and Laurie Anderson found it some years ago.

Blackberry Scallop Ceviche

Blackberry Ketchup

Chinook Winery Washington Semillon (Topaz)
This delightful, refreshing dry white wine with a typical fresh-cut-grass character is made by two of the most delightful and refreshing Washington winemakers, Kay Simon and Clay Mackey. Its fruity dryness nicely off-sets the citrusy quality of the ceviche and the clean taste of the scallops.

8 c blackberries
2 shallots, minced
1 yellow onion, chopped
2 tsp dried tarragon
2 tsp dried marjoram
1 tsp dried rosemary
juice and zest of **1** lemon
¾ c balsamic vinegar
½ c sugar
1 tsp salt
½ tsp pepper

Combine all ingredients except the salt and pepper in a large sauce pan. Cover and bring to a boil. Reduce the heat and simmer for 10 minutes.

Cool slightly, then purée the ketchup in a blender and strain it through a medium sieve into a clean sauce pan, pressing it to retrieve as much purée as possible.

Add the salt and pepper and reduce over low heat to 4 cups.

Makes 4 cups.

Use this ketchup as you would tomato ketchup. It is great with poultry and meats, and will hold in the refrigerator for at least six months.

Blackberry Scallop Ceviche

Blackberry Marinated Onions

4 red onions
2 c blackberry vinegar (or raspberry vinegar)
½ c honey

Peel the onions and slice them as thin as possible.

Mix together the vinegar and honey. Add the onions and marinate overnight at room temperature—they will become a vibrant pink color.

Refrigerate. They will keep well for 2 weeks.

Makes 4 cups.

These onions are a wonderful addition to salads, as a "bed" for meat or fish entrées or as an accompaniment to pâtés. You may use the marinade over again and keep a "stash" of the onions in the refrigerator. We have used them as a bed for POACHED PEPPER LIME OYSTERS IN SAUCE *and* BLACKBERRY SCALLOP CEVICHE; *you'll find both of these recipes included in this collection.*

In a very short time after opening the restaurant, we saw our dreams for The Shoalwater begin to come true. On July 10, 1982, the phone rang. "This is Charles Michener calling from Newsweek Magazine *in New York. I'm doing a story on new up-and-coming restaurants around the country. Is the owner in?"*

SPRING NETTLE SOUP

Columbia Winery
Washington Gewürztraminer
Gewürztraminer, besides being one of the most mispronounced wines in the biz (a source of much backroom amusement in the restaurant and wine trades), is a fascinating wine variety due to the range of flavors it can produce. Columbia's David Lake produces a lovely dry and spicy wine (somewhat reminiscent of wildflowers, making it a natural to accompany a nettle soup) in the tradition of the finest Alsatian wines of that type.

1 lb fresh young nettles
1 yellow onion, peeled & sliced
3 stalks celery, chopped
2 shallots, minced
1 Tb butter
2 c chicken stock
1 tsp dried tarragon
1 tsp dried chervil
2 c heavy cream
¼ c fresh lemon juice
1 tsp salt
½ tsp pepper
edible flowers, for garnish

Use tongs or gloves to put the nettles into a sink full of water to clean them. Lift them out with the tongs, shake them lightly and put directly into a large sauce pan. *No need to add water; there will be enough on them from being cleaned.* Cover and steam slightly over medium heat until well wilted. Remove from heat and set aside.

In another sauce pan sauté the onion, celery and shallots in the butter until soft.

Add the nettles, chicken stock, tarragon and chervil. Bring it to a boil, reduce the heat and simmer for 15 minutes. Purée the nettle mixture in a food processor, strain it through a medium sieve and return it to a clean sauce pan.

Add the cream and lemon juice and heat through, but *do not boil.* Season with salt and pepper.

A nice garnish for this Spring soup is the petals of edible flowers such as bright orange calendula or small English daisies (the kind that grow in lawns!).

Makes 6 servings.

Lemon Chicken Soup

5 c chicken stock
1/4 c fresh lemon juice
1/4 c carrot, shredded
1/4 c onion, chopped
1/4 c celery, chopped
2 tsp salt
1 tsp white pepper
2 Tb butter, softened
2 Tb flour
4 egg yolks
1/2 c heavy cream
1/4 c cooked white rice
1/2 c cooked chicken, diced
lemon slices, for garnish

Chateau Ste. Michelle Johannisberg Riesling
This is the wine that literally put Washington State on the modern day wine map and continues to be one of this well-known winery's most popular. Fruity, floral, and still finished with a hint of sweetness in the German Spätlese style, this fresh-tasting, easy-drinking wine is a clean accompaniment to all manner of light dishes such as this soup.

Combine stock, lemon juice, carrot, onion, celery, salt and pepper in a large sauce pan. Bring to a boil over high heat, reduce the heat, cover partially and simmer until the vegetables are tender, about 20 minutes.

Blend the butter and flour until smooth and add to the hot soup, a bit at a time, stirring constantly. Simmer for 10 minutes, continuing to stir.

In an electric mixer, beat the yolks with the cream until blended. Reduce the speed and mix in the hot soup, a bit at a time.

Return the soup to the sauce pan and bring to a low boil. Add the rice and chicken. Season to taste.

Ladle into bowls and garnish with lemon slices.

If you prefer a more tart soup, add another table-spoon of fresh lemon juice.

Makes 6 cups.

STURGEON AND MUSSELS EN COCOTTE

Seaview's neighboring towns of Long Beach and Ilwaco were originally platted by wise speculators but Seaview "just growed" and even today is unincorporated.

18 Penn Cove mussels, scrubbed & de-bearded

1¼ c white wine

3 tsp butter

2 lb boneless sturgeon fillet, cut in ¼-inch slices across the grain

1½ c BOURBON VIN BLANC

¾ c APPLE SHALLOT GLAZE

Steam the mussels open in ½ cup of the wine in a covered sauce pan. Set aside and let cool.

Grease 6 custard cups and line the bottom and sides with the sturgeon, filling the middle of the cup with about 3 each of the mussels (in the shells for color, if you wish). *You should end up with sturgeon-wrapped mussels, with the open tips of the mussels peeking out the top.* Top each with 2 tablespoons of white wine and ½ teaspoon butter.

Place the cups in a hot water bath and bake in a preheated 500° oven until the sturgeon is just done, about 8 to 10 minutes.

Pool ¼ cup of BOURBON VIN BLANC on each plate. Invert the cups to drain, then turn them back over and unmold them on top of the sauce. Use a squeeze bottle to swirl the APPLE SHALLOT GLAZE from the top of the mussels into the sauce.

You may also use just the mussel meat with the sturgeon and use the shells for holding very colorful purées such as squash, carrot, beet, pea or broccoli. Very pretty presentation!

Makes 6 servings.

Sturgeon and Mussels en Cocotte

Apple Shallot Glaze

2 Tb butter

2 shallots, minced

4 c apple cider

2 c Shoalwater Shrimp Stock

2 c chicken stock

¼ c brandy

¼ c balsamic vinegar

Columbia Crest Columbia Valley Sauvignon Blanc
Clean, crisp and classically herbaceous, Doug Gore's Sauvignon Blanc from Columbia Crest is a beautifully-balanced version of the varietal which enhances (and does not interfere) with the elegant, stately flavor of the Columbia River sturgeon and the sea-saltiness of the mussels which Cheri has so elegantly paired in this dish.

Melt 1 tablespoon of the butter in a medium sauce pan and slowly sauté the shallots until golden.

Add the cider and stocks, turn the heat to high and reduce to 1 cup. Strain out the shallots and return to a clean pan. Add the brandy and balsamic vinegar and reduce to ¾ cup, about 2 more minutes. Remove from the heat and cool slightly. *This should have the look of maple syrup—dark and thick. If it is too thin after it cools, return it to high heat and reduce it for 1 to 2 more minutes. Be watchful: the glaze will scorch and caramelize very quickly at this point.* Cool, then put the glaze into a plastic ketchup squeeze bottle and set aside.

We modify this glaze for use on pork tenderloin by substituting chicken stock or veal stock for the shrimp stock.

Makes ¾ cup.

Sturgeon and Mussels en Cocotte

Bourbon Vin Blanc

In 1983 we added a second dining room to the 45-seat area we had taken over in 1981. Joining in on an expansion of The Shelburne Inn, we were able to increase our ability to serve our growing clientele at the same time the Inn increased its capacity by one third.

½ c bourbon
2 c white wine
2½ c chicken stock
2 c heavy cream

In a sauce pan, reduce the bourbon and wine over high heat to 1 cup. Reserve.

In a second pan, reduce the stock over high heat to 1 cup. Reserve.

In a third pan, reduce the cream over medium heat to 1 cup, watching carefully that the cream does not boil over.

Combine the reductions into one sauce pan. Reduce gently over medium-low heat to 1½ cups. Hold in a container set in warm water until ready to use.

This is a classic Vin Blanc *sauce with bourbon added. It goes well with seafood or chicken, particularly smoked poultry. It should be used as soon as it is made—reheating it usually causes it to break.*

Makes 1½ cups.

NORTHWEST CIOPPINO

2 onions, finely chopped
4 cloves garlic, minced
12 sprigs parsley, finely chopped
½ c olive oil
6 c roma tomatoes, peeled, seeded & coarsely chopped
3 c tomato sauce
2 c red wine
2 c water
4 Tb red wine vinegar
1½ c fish stock (or clam nectar)
1½ tsp each basil, rosemary, marjoram & oregano
salt & pepper, to taste
24 steamer clams
½ c clarified butter
24 large scallops (about **¾ lb**)
24 medium shrimp (about **1 lb**)
1½ lb fresh fish

Columbia Red Willow Vineyard (Milestone) Merlot
Bring out the big guns—but disguise their punch in soft gloves. Again, David Lake manages to carefully craft a wine which has lots of dark berry flavors but goes down very smoothly, even at a relatively young age. In the absence of a plethora of Italian wine varietals in the Northwest —we have one, Peter Dow's excellent Cavatappi Nebbiolo—this is as good a match as I can come up with to accompany that great "Italian"dish—from San Francisco's North Beach district—Cioppino.

Sauté onion, garlic and parsley in olive oil over medium heat until onion is transparent.

Add tomatoes, tomato sauce, wine, water, vinegar, stock, herbs, salt and pepper. Bring to a boil, reduce heat and simmer for 40 minutes. *The Cioppino base freezes wonderfully at this point.*

In a separate large sauce pan, sauté the clams in the clarified butter until they open. Turn down the heat and add the rest of the seafood all at once. Sauté lightly until about halfway cooked.

Add the Cioppino base and bring the soup to a boil to heat through and finish cooking the seafood.

Dish into 8 bowls, making sure everyone has some

continued...

NORTHWEST CIOPPINO

...continued

of everything! Accompany with garlic bread croutons (top slices of buttered French bread with minced garlic and Parmesan cheese, then lightly brown them under the broiler).

The stock for this Cioppino makes a wonderful sauce for spaghetti when thickened with a bit of tomato paste.

Makes 8 servings

Shoalwater Seafood Fettuccine

3 Tb unsalted butter
$\frac{1}{2}$ red onion, julienned
2 tsp garlic, minced
4 oz fresh crab meat
4 oz fresh shrimp
3 oz Ouzo
1 c heavy cream
3 c fettuccine, cooked
2 tsp dried parsley
1 tsp salt
$\frac{1}{2}$ tsp pepper
1 c Parmesan cheese

Melt butter in a medium sauce pan. Sauté the onion and garlic until translucent.

Add the crab and shrimp. Toss to combine and heat through. Add the Ouzo and let it reduce enough to evaporate the alcohol.

Add the cream and pasta. Stir once to combine, then cook until the sauce has thickened and darkened in color.

Add the parsley, salt, pepper and $\frac{3}{4}$ cup of the Parmesan. Stir gently until the cheese is incorporated.

Place on plates and top with the remaining cheese.

Makes 2 servings.

Columbia Wykoff Vineyards Chardonnay

Ann and I went to Whitman College in Walla Walla with David Wykoff, who was then working hard on his pre-law degree. He did go on to become a successful attorney, we hear, and is now obviously pursuing the next logical consequence of that career, growing exceptional grapes. Count on David Lake to extract the most flavor from Wykoff's Chardonnay grapes (the '89 is ambrosial!). This ever-popular Fettuccine preparation needs a match like this one.

This recipe works best with home-made noodles. Quick and easy to prepare, it should be accompanied with fresh French bread and a salad of wild and garden greens.

RAVIOLI APERTO

Chinook Columbia Valley Chardonnay
The well-respected Chinook winemakers produce their dry white wines to bring out the cleanest flavor of the respective grapes, down-playing oak and other "enhancers" to focus on the varieties' actual flavors. This lovely, subtle dish deserves such a perfect match.

For the plain pasta:

2⁄3 c semolina flour
3⁄4 c white flour
1 tsp water
3 eggs

For the mushroom pasta:

2⁄3 c semolina flour
3⁄4 c white flour
2 tsp water
3 eggs
1 oz dried mushrooms, ground to a dust

For the filling:

1 oz dried mushrooms, soaked 1 hour in **1 c** hot water
1⁄3 c ROASTED GARLIC
1⁄4 tsp salt
2 Tb chives, chopped

For the assembly:

2 c MUSHROOM GARLIC CREAM SAUCE

To make the pasta, you need a pasta machine—hand-cranked is fine.

For each pasta: Combine the flours (*for the mushroom pasta, add the mushroom dust to the flours.*) and create a well in the center. Combine the water with the eggs and pour into the well. With a fork, whisk the eggs, slowly pulling in flour from the sides of the well, until a firm dough begins to form. Knead the dough with the heel of your hand for about 5 minutes, wrap it tightly in plastic and let it sit for 30 minutes.

Working with a third of the dough at a time, roll the dough through a pasta machine, until quite thin. Trim to 2½ to 3 inch squares. Lay the squares on a

continued...

Ravioli Aperto

...continued

sheet pan and cover with plastic wrap. Place in the refrigerator.

To create an interesting design, place small, very thin leaves of parsley, chives or thin slices of mushroom at 2-inch intervals along the length of a pasta sheet. Top with a second sheet of pasta and slowly pass the double sheet through the rollers to achieve a subtle leaf or mushroom shape. Trim to size and refrigerate as above.

For the filling, drain the mushrooms and reserve the liquid.

In a food processor, pulse the soaked mushrooms, the roasted garlic, salt and chives to form a coarse purée. *You may need to add a bit of the soaking liquid to moisten the purée.*

Before assembling the ravioli, heat the purée in the microwave or in a sauté pan over medium heat.

In a large sauce pan, bring salted water to a boil and add the pasta squares. Cook until *al dente,* no more than 2 minutes.

To serve, divide the PORCINI & ROASTED GARLIC CREAM SAUCE between the plates and top with the mushroom pasta squares. Put a tablespoon of the purée on top of each pasta square, then place a plain pasta square over the filling at an angle to the mushroom square.

Garnish with chives, MARINATED GRILLED BOLETUS mushrooms (see recipe) or whole ROASTED GARLIC.

Makes 6 to 8 servings of one ravioli per serving.

Some of our wild mushrooms, the local equivalent of the Italian porcini, coupled with everybody's favorite, garlic, in a Roasted Garlic Cream Sauce, provide the base for this rich treat. While we serve this dish as a first course in a banquet meal, don't miss a chance to serve Ravioli Aperto as an entrée. Step by step from Roasted Garlic, through the cream sauce, to the final assembly, Ravioli Aperto will be a pleasure to the home chef and guests alike.

RAVIOLI APERTO

PORCINI & ROASTED GARLIC CREAM SAUCE

1 oz dried boletus mushrooms (also called porcini)

2 c hot water

2 c veal demi-glace (**4 c** SHOALWATER VEAL STOCK reduced to **2 c**)

⅔ c red wine

2 oz ROASTED GARLIC

1½ c heavy cream

4 Tb butter, chilled & cut into bits

Combine the mushrooms and water in a heatproof pan. Let it sit over lowest heat for at least 30 minutes.

Strain them, reserving both the water and the mushrooms.

If you soak the mushrooms overnight at room temperature, the broth will be even stronger.

Combine the demi-glace, red wine and mushroom broth in a sauce pan. Bring to a boil and reduce to ¾ cup.

In a blender, purée the ROASTED GARLIC with a bit of the reduction. Add the purée and cream to the sauce pan with the reduction, stirring well. Bring to a boil and reduce to 2 cups.

Whisk in the chilled butter, bit by bit. Hold over warm water until ready to serve.

Use the reserved mushrooms to prepare the stuffing for RAVIOLI APERTO, or chop them fine for combining in stir-fries, omelettes or crêpes.

Makes 2 cups.

Roasted Garlic

1 lb whole garlic bulbs

3 Tb olive oil

Cut the tops, not the root end, off the garlic bulbs to expose the cloves inside. Place them in a shallow roasting pan and drizzle each bulb with olive oil.

Cover the pan with foil and seal the edges. Roast in a preheated 350° oven until the cloves pop up, about 1 to 1¼ hours.

Serve either the whole bulb, or pop the cloves out.

Makes about 1 cup.

You may hold this garlic in the refrigerator covered with olive oil, almost indefinitely. Have fun with these. They give a rich, earthy flavor to mayonnaise, are great added to soups or pestos, or can be mashed and spread on toasted French bread and eaten "au naturel!"

Marinated Grilled Boletus

1 lb fresh boletus mushrooms

2 c olive oil

1 c peanut oil

1 c balsamic vinegar

¼ c brandy

1½ Tb garlic, minced

1½ Tb fresh chervil, finely chopped

2 tsp salt

1 tsp pepper

Slice the boletus into ½ -inch "steaks," that is, slice a cross section of the mushrooms about ½ -inch thick.

Mix the remaining ingredients in a large mixing bowl.

Lay the steaks into the marinade, making sure they all get moistened. Marinate for at least 4 hours.

Drain and grill until they're heated through. *Be sure not to overcook.*

Makes 4 servings.

GRILLED LAMB CHOPS WITH GREEN PEPPER

Chateau Ste. Michelle Cold Creek Vineyard Cabernet Sauvignon

Quietly but surely, Chateau Ste. Michelle is developing a remarkable track record for producing a line of excellent premium, single-vineyard reserve red wines. Cold Creek Vineyard consistently produces Cabernets of intensity, power and richness. A well-aged sample will stand up nicely to the full flavors Cheri brings out in this lovely dish.

1 c olive oil
2½ c red wine
2 tsp garlic, minced (4 cloves)
4 sprigs rosemary (or 4 tsp dried)
1 small green pepper, sliced
2 tsp black pepper
6 6-8 oz lamb chops
3 shallots, minced
4 Tb butter
1½ c lamb stock
(or SHOALWATER VEAL STOCK)
¾ c GREEN PEPPERCORN & HONEY MUSTARD
1½ c heavy cream

Whisk together olive oil, 2 cups of the red wine, garlic, 3 sprigs of the rosemary, green pepper and black pepper. Add the lamb chops, cover them and refrigerate overnight.

Sauté the shallots in 2 tablespoons of the butter until they turn soft. Add the remaining ½ cup of red wine, the remaining sprig of rosemary and the stock and boil until the liquid is reduced by half.

Strain into a clean sauté pan. Add the mustard, whisking well to combine and then reduce again by half.

Add the cream and reduce until the sauce begins to thicken. Add the remaining 2 tablespoons of butter and hold the sauce over warm water while you cook the lamb chops.

Remove the lamb chops from the marinade and pat dry. Grill the chops until resilient and barely pink. Serve with the mustard sauce.

Makes 6 servings.

GREEN PEPPERCORN & HONEY MUSTARD

½ c mustard seeds
3 Tb Coleman's dry mustard
½ c water
2 small green peppers (about **13 oz** total)
2 Tb green peppercorns in water
¼ c balsamic vinegar
¼ c honey
2 tsp salt
2 Tb dried rosemary (or **¼ c** fresh)

Combine the mustard seeds, dry mustard and water in a blender or food processor and process until it resembles a coarse purée. Let it sit, uncovered, for at least 3 hours at room temperature.

Roast the green peppers under a broiler or over a gas flame or grill, turning until all sides have blackened and blistered. Place in a plastic bag to cool, then peel and seed the peppers.

In a food processor, blend the roasted peppers, green peppercorns, vinegar, honey, salt and rosemary. Add the mustard mixture and blend well.

Cover and allow it to sit overnight. *This will keep indefinitely in the refrigerator or at room temperature.*

Makes 3 cups.

As with all mustards, this makes a great gift and is easy to put together. If you would like to keep the mustard hot, keep it refrigerated. Leave it tightly capped at room temperature if you prefer it to gradually mellow.

CHOCOLATE PEAR CAKE

Whidbey's Washington Port
Chateau Ste. Michelle got its start unglamorously as the off-shoot of a company whose claim to fame was fortified berry wines. Nostalgically, they hold on to the the largest lingonberry farm in the country on Whidbey Island, where they now produce the refined lingonberry liqueur and a flavorful port-style wine made from sweetened and fortified Cabernet Sauvignon. And port and chocolate simply works!

½ c butter
10 oz semisweet chocolate
1 c coffee
½ c unsweetened cocoa powder
1 ½ c all purpose flour
1 tsp baking soda
¼ tsp baking powder
¼ tsp salt
1 ¼ c sugar
2 eggs
4 Tb pear liqueur (or pear brandy)
1 pear, peeled, cored & cut into ½-inch dice
¾ c heavy cream
1 pear, peeled, cored & pureed
1 recipe CRÈME ANGLAISE (see variation following)
1 pear, peeled & sliced, for garnish

Melt the butter and 2 ounces of the chocolate with the coffee, then stir in the cocoa. Place the mixture in a mixing bowl.

Sift together the flour, baking soda, baking powder, salt and sugar. On low speed, add the dry ingredients to the wet, mixing until the dry ingredients are moistened.

Add the eggs one at a time, mixing well after each addition. Add 2 tablespoons of the pear liqueur and gently fold in the diced pear.

Grease and line a 10-inch cake pan with parchment. Pour in the batter and check to see that the pears are evenly distributed in the pan. Bake in a preheated 350° oven until the cake begins to shrink away from the sides of the pan, about 25 to 30 minutes.

continued...

CHOCOLATE PEAR CAKE

...continued

Remove from the pan and allow to cool.

For the glaze, melt the remaining 8 ounces of chocolate with the cream (a microwave works well for this; it takes about 2 minutes).

Stir in the pear purée and the remaining 2 tablespoons of pear brandy. Cool until it has begun to thicken enough to spread over the cake.

Glaze the cake and refrigerate briefly to set.

Serve garnished with sliced pears and a pear CRÈME ANGLAISE. *To make pear CRÈME ANGLAISE, follow the recipe for CRÈME ANGLAISE, substituting pear brandy for the liqueur and stir in 1 pear, seeded and pureed, at the end.*

Makes one 10-inch cake.

Pumpkin Sherry Flan

Columbia Winery Cellarmaster's Reserve Johannisberg Riesling
Columbia Winery produces a lot of different wines and does them all remarkably well. This low-alcohol Riesling is produced with some (but not too much) residual sweetness in the German Auslese tradition, and serves nicely to complement a lighter dessert like this flan.

1½ c sugar
1 c pumpkin purée (fresh or canned)
¾ tsp cinnamon
¼ tsp ginger
½ tsp salt
4 eggs, beaten
1¾ c half and half
¼ c Sherry
whipped cream, for garnish

Heat 1 cup of the sugar in a sauce pan over high heat. Stir constantly, breaking up lumps of sugar as they form. *Work quickly once the sugar begins to liquify—it will burn easily.* Cook only until it turns a rich golden color—*do not overcook*—it will continue to cook once removed from the heat.

Pour the caramelized sugar into each of six 6-ounce custard cups, swirling each cup to coat the sides evenly and pouring any excess into the next cup *(you may need to reheat the caramel if it stiffens).* Allow to cool.

Combine the pumpkin, remaining ½ cup of sugar, spices and salt in a mixing bowl. Add the beaten eggs, blending well. Mix in the half and half, then the Sherry.

Divide the mixture among the custard dishes. Place the cups in a large roasting pan and fill the pan with enough water to come halfway up the sides of the custard cups.

Bake in a preheated 350° oven until a knife inserted in the middle comes out clean, about 30 to 35 minutes.

Allow them to cool in the water bath to room

continued...

Pumpkin Sherry Flan

...continued

temperature, then take them out of the water. Chill completely.

To serve, run a narrow-bladed knife around the edge of the cup and invert each over a plate. Scrape the excess caramel over the flan and top with whipped cream.

Makes 6 servings.

Eyrie
Amity
Tualatin

Marinated Prawns on Spaghettini Piccata
Eyrie Vineyards Willamette Valley Chardonnay

OR

Asian Crab Cakes
Tualatin Vineyards Willamette Valley Gewürztraminer

Braided Salmon & Sturgeon in Caviar Beurre Blanc
Amity Vineyards Willamette Valley Dry White Riesling

OR

Grilled Scallops with Orange & Gin Sabayon Sauce
Tualatin Vineyards Private Reserve Chardonnay

Gewürztraminer Granité

Asparagus & Shrimp Risotto
Amity Vineyards Willamette Valley Chardonnay

Daubé of Quail & Morels
Eyrie Vineyards Reserve Pinot Noir

Lemon Chess Tart
Tualatin Vineyards Late Harvest Chardonnay

OR

Ann's Bread Pudding
Amity Vineyards Late Harvest White Riesling

EYRIE
AMITY
TUALATIN

May 15, 1976. It takes about three hours to travel by train from Paris to the ancient town of Beaune in the heart of the Burgundy region. As the train passed Dijon, leaving its endless yellow mustard fields, and we headed south into the famous wine region for the first time, I got increasingly excited. The familiar town/wine appellation signs whizzed by beside the tracks — Fixin, Nuits, Gevrey, Morey — all names I knew well from the wines I had served or tasted over many years. I grabbed the well-thumbed copy of Hugh Johnson's World Atlas of Wine from my carry-on and found the right page. Dashing back and forth across the train, open book in hand, I began to identify the famous vineyards. I was, as our daughters Jenny and Michelle would say, pumped.

I was still excited when we arrived in Beaune. The taxicab squeezed down a one-lane cobblestone street lined with buildings centuries old and stopped in front of a stone doorway framed by wrought iron shutters and identified only by a small brass sign, Hotel Le Cep. We found our way through massive antiques to the front desk, where we completed the necessary paperwork. Then a petite Spanish maid carried our bags to an upstairs room and pointed out the bathroom down the hall. The room, furnished with comfortable antiques, had tall ceilings and big French doors opening onto a small balcony. When we stepped outside, we could see a small patisserie just across the street.

After a quick nap, we went down to the tiny bar and enjoyed an aperitif and a palate tickler before we went to dinner in the vaulted, low-ceilinged dining room. The fare was traditionally Burgundian, using local recipes and ingredients, and accompanied by an extensive list of fine local wines. Just as I dozed off to sleep that night I said to Ann, "Wouldn't it be great to own something like this some time?"

June 25, 1981. We were enjoying a day off at home in Seattle when the phone rang. It was our friend Blaine Walker calling, he said, from Long Beach.

"You're where? California?"

"No, down on the southwest Washington coast."

"Oh. So what's up?"

"You know that restaurant in a small country inn you've been talking about wanting for so long? I think I've found it — and it's for sale!"

MARINATED PRAWNS ON SPAGHETTINI PICCATA

1 c parsley, leaves only
4 Tb capers
2 ½ Tb garlic, minced
½ tsp kosher salt
¾ c + 2 Tb olive oil
juice of **2** lemons (about **½ c**)
2 lb prawns, peeled & deveined, tail left on
2 red onions, julienned
½ c pinenuts, toasted
2 Tb oregano
6 roma tomatoes, diced
6 portions cooked spaghettini (al dente)

Eyrie Vineyards Willamette Valley Chardonnay
David Lett is considered the "grand-daddy" of Oregon's currrent wine boom, having been one of the first to set roots (literally and figuratively) in the Willamette Valley, back in 1965. He set out to produce great examples of his favorite Burgundian varietals, Chardonnay and Pinot Noir, and has set the pace and tone for them now in Oregon. The full flavors of his Chardonnay do nice things for the richness of this shellfish pasta.

In a blender, purée the parsley, 1 tablespoon of the capers, 1½ teaspoons of the garlic and salt. With the machine running, add ½ cup of olive oil in a slow stream. Then add the juice of 1 lemon.

Place prawns in a bowl in layers with the marinade. Marinate for 24 hours.

Heat remaining 6 tablespoons of oil in a sauce pan. Sauté onions, pinenuts and the remaining 2 tablespoons of garlic. When onions begin to soften, add oregano, tomatoes, remaining ¼ cup of lemon juice and the remaining 3 tablespoons of capers. Heat through.

Add the pasta then toss until the liquid is evaporated and the pasta is hot. Divide among 6 plates.

Grill (or sauté) the prawns briefly on both sides until they are just cooked through. Arrange prawns on the top of the pasta. Serve immediately.

Makes 6 servings.

Because this dish uses olive oil as its only fat, it is an excellent low-fat and low-cholesterol entrée.

ASIAN CRAB CAKES

Tualatin Vineyards Willamette Valley Gewürztraminer
Bill and Virginia Fuller are two of the most gregarious members of the Oregon wine industry, and produce some of that state's most gregarious and fine wines (all from their own estate vineyards). Their Gewürztraminer is fresh, dry and spicy and, characteristically, works beautifully with the Asian quality of this dish.

2 c cracker meal
1 lb crab meat, drained well
1 green onion, finely chopped
½ sweet red pepper, finely chopped
1 lb Gruyère cheese, grated
1½ tsp sesame oil
1 egg white
1 Tb sake
1 Tb soy sauce
1 Tb ginger root, grated
½ tsp garlic, minced
¼ tsp black pepper
peanut oil, for frying
2 c RED PEPPER & GINGER MAYONNAISE
Chive blossoms, for garnish

Set 1½ cup of the cracker meal aside for breading.

Combine the remaining ½ cup of cracker meal with all of the remaining ingredients except the peanut oil and mayonnaise. Shape into ½-ounce patties, carefully forming the edges, and pat into the reserved cracker meal. Set them aside.

Coat the bottom of a frying pan with a thin layer of peanut oil. Set it over medium heat and sauté the cakes until golden on both sides.

Pool ¼ cup of RED PEPPER & GINGER MAYONNAISE on each plate and top with 2 cakes. Garnish with chive blossoms, bits of red pepper or green onion strands.

Makes 8 servings.

RED PEPPER & GINGER MAYONNAISE

2 sweet red peppers, roasted, peeled & seeded

1 c mayonnaise

2 ½ tsp sesame oil

3 Tb sake

1 tsp soy sauce

1 tsp garlic, minced

2 Tb ginger root, grated (or 1 piece 1 inch in diameter by 2 inches long)

This mayonnaise sauce is an excellent dip for vegetables or a quick sauce for fish. Personally, I think it's great with beef fondue, steaks and carpaccio.

Combine all the ingredients and purée in a food processor or blender until smooth. *If you prefer a smoother sauce, pass the mayonnaise through a fine-mesh strainer.*

Makes 2 cups.

BRAIDED SALMON & STURGEON IN CAVIAR BEURRE BLANC

Amity Vineyards Willamette Valley Dry White Riesling
When Myron Redford makes wine from traditional German and Alsatian varietals, such as Riesling and Gewürztraminer, he is appropriately "most correct" and consistently turns out some of the region's loveliest examples of what these grapes can do at their driest. This is another delightful combination of food and wine, where the balance of flavors all-around is a remarkable triumph.

4 Tb shallots, minced
¾ c white wine vinegar
1½ c white wine
1 c butter
1 16-oz salmon fillet
1 16-oz sturgeon fillet
2 Tb caviar
white pepper, to taste

Combine the shallots, vinegar and ½ cup of wine in a small sauce pan. Simmer until reduced to approximately 2 tablespoons.

Remove the pan from the heat and whip in the butter, a bit at a time, until all of the butter has been incorporated. Strain the sauce into a bowl. Place the bowl into a warm water bath to hold.

Cut the salmon and sturgeon into pieces ½ by ½ by 8 inches long (use two 4-inch lengths if you need to), by first slicing ½-inch thick pieces lengthwise, then cutting the slices into ½-inch widths.

Braid 2 of one fish and 1 of the other by laying the 3 strips side by side and pulling the right hand strip over the center strip, left hand over the center, and so on. You may leave the braid long or form it into a wreath shape.

Place the fish braids on a baking sheet, cover with the remaining 1 cup of wine and bake in a preheated 500° oven for 10 minutes.

Remove the fish and place on a serving platter.

continued...

Braided Salmon & Sturgeon in Caviar Beurre Blanc

...continued

Add the caviar and pepper to the warm sauce and mix well. Ladle the sauce over the fish and serve immediately.

Makes 6 servings.

Several years ago we renovated the restaurant's original, tiny, home-style kitchen. We could finally provide our staff with truly professional equipment and enough storage space to let us produce the quality dining we had aspired to from the beginning.

GRILLED SCALLOPS
WITH
ORANGE & GIN SABAYON SAUCE

Scallops take subtle flavors so well, and this preparation which includes the Orange-Gin Sabayon Sauce (its recipe is on the next page) is one of our favorites. We are constantly surprised and delighted by the ideas that come out of our kitchen and out of our staff meetings. The chef may traditionally be the virtuoso in the kitchen, but at The Shoalwater, each dinner comes from the work of a balanced kitchen and dining room staff.

2 tsp juniper berries, crushed
½ c gin
2 c orange juice
½ tsp cinnamon
¼ tsp cardamom
2 tsp rose water
2 lb scallops
3 c ORANGE GIN SABAYON SAUCE

Pulse the juniper berries in a blender or food processor until finely ground. Add the gin, orange juice, spices and rose water. Pulse until blended.

Divide the scallops into 6 portions and thread onto bamboo skewers.

Lay the skewers into a shallow baking dish and pour the marinade over them. Cover and refrigerate overnight.

Grill the scallops on a barbecue, basting frequently with the marinade, until the scallops are heated through, about 1 to 2 minutes on each side.

Remove from the flame and serve with ORANGE GIN SABAYON SAUCE.

Makes 6 servings.

HOGUE
THE HOGUE CELLARS

GRILLED SCALLOPS

ORANGE & GIN SABAYON SAUCE

zest and juice of **1** orange
1/4 tsp cardamom
1/2 tsp cinnamon
1 tsp juniper berries, ground
1/4 c gin
3/4 c orange juice concentrate
3/4 c water
1 Tb rose water
1/2 c butter
6 egg yolks
1 tsp salt

Combine all the ingredients except the egg yolks and salt in the top of a double boiler over—*not in*—boiling water. Heat until the butter melts, stirring to combine.

Add the egg yolks and whisk continuously until the sauce begins to thicken and become somewhat fluffy. Add salt.

Remove from the heat and hold in a warm water bath until ready to use.

Makes 2 1/2 cups.

Tualatin Vineyards Private Reserve Chardonnay
Bill Fuller has always been one of the most honest winemakers in this business, actually pricing his wines in each vintage to match their quality rather than the market. This Chardonnay, in the 1989 vintage especially, is priced right up there, but is equally flavored and well-balanced. The richness of this wine's flavors fits right in with the intensity of the egg-based orange-flavored sauce.

GEWÜRZTRAMINER GRANITÉ

1 c sugar
1 c water
1 bottle Gerwürztraminer wine
juice of **1** lemon
mint sprigs, for garnish

Bring sugar and water to a boil in a small sauce pan. Boil for 1 minute, then remove from heat and allow to cool. Refrigerate.

When the syrup is cold, add the wine and lemon juice. Place mixture in a 9 by 13 inch pan and put in the freezer.

As crystals begin to form around the edges of the pan, run a whisk around the edge to break them up. Return to the freezer.

Continue whisking every hour or so, until the entire pan is frozen into crystals.

Serve garnished with a sprig of mint and a flower.

Makes 10 to 12 servings as a palate cleanser, or 4 to 6 as a dessert.

Asparagus & Shrimp Risotto

½ lb asparagus
3 Tb butter
2 shallots, minced
¼ tsp salt
⅛ tsp black pepper
¼ c white wine
1 c Arborio rice, uncooked
3 c Shoalwater Shrimp Stock, held just below a boil
⅓ c Parmesan cheese
2 Tb parsley, chopped
½ lb shrimp meat, cooked
zest of **1** orange

Amity Vineyards Willamette Valley Chardonnay
This crisp Chardonnay, made in stainless steel and aged slightly in wood, yields the green-apple and pear tastes of the grape itself to complement the fresh vegetable flavors of the season's first asparagus.

Slice the asparagus into ⅛-inch pieces, reserving 2 inches of each tip and discarding the coarse ends.

In a medium sauce pan, sauté the shallots in 2 tablespoons of the butter, then add the asparagus pieces (not the reserved tips), salt and pepper and cook for 1 minute. Add the wine and cook until the liquid has evaporated.

Add the rice and 1 cup of the hot stock. Stir once and cook over medium heat until the liquid is absorbed, about 6 minutes. Add another cup of stock and again cook until the liquid is absorbed.

Add the remaining cup of stock and cook for about 8 minutes. The rice is ready when it is creamy with slightly *al dente* grains.

Meanwhile, steam the reserved asparagus tips.

Stir the Parmesan, parsley, shrimp, orange zest and remaining tablespoon of butter into the rice and serve garnished with the steamed asparagus tips.

Makes 6 cups.

DAUBÉ OF QUAIL & MORELS

__Eyrie Vineyards Reserve Pinot Noir__
Here's where David Lett lets it "all hang out"—in great years, like 1983, 1985, and 1988, he bottles little time bombs of flavor in his reserve Pinot Noirs. Drink the oldest one you can afford; they need time to release all the fruit and display all the elegance and balance he packs into them. And enjoy the richness of the quail and morel flavors even more because of this wine choice.

2 Tb butter, melted
2 Tb flour
1 pt fresh pearl onions
1 lb bacon, cut into ½-inch pieces
6 quail, trussed
1 c Merlot
4 c chicken stock, reduced to **2** c
salt & pepper, to taste
½ c parsley, finely chopped
2 tsp garlic, minced
1 lb fresh morel mushrooms

Prepare a roux by mixing flour into melted butter over low heat until it thickens.

Remove the skins from the onions by trimming both ends, dipping in boiling water for 2 minutes and squeezing them. (They will pop out into your fingers.)

Cook the bacon pieces just until they are crisp. Set bacon aside.

Brown the quail in the bacon grease. Set them in a casserole with the bacon pieces.

Drain the bacon grease and deglaze the pan with the Merlot. Soften the roux with some of the chicken stock and add it to the pan. Add the remaining stock and stir until smooth. Season with salt and pepper.

Sprinkle the onions, parsley, garlic and mushrooms over the quail and pour the liquid over the top.

Cook covered in a preheated 500° oven until done, about 20 minutes.

Remove and untie the quail. Strain the sauce.

continued...

Daubé of Quail & Morels

...continued

To serve, spoon the bacon, onions and mushrooms onto a plate, set the quail on top and pour the sauce over it all. Accompany it with your favorite rice.

Makes 6 servings.

In the fall of 1987 we opened the cozy Heron & Beaver Pub where we feature regional beers and light fare as well as a full bar and a place for a friendly conversation.

LEMON CHESS TART

PÂTE BRISÉE

Tualatin Vineyards
Late Harvest Chardonnay
This is a delightful little aberrant wine. Bill Fuller makes this from some very ripe Chardonnay grapes which he vinifies up to a certain degree of alcohol, arresting the fermentation and allowing a certain amount of residual sugar to remain, producing an unusual wine with a Riesling sweetness but a Chardonnay flavor. A good match to the sweet-tart quality of Lemon Chess Tart.

3 ⅓ c all purpose flour
¼ c sugar
1 c butter, chilled & cut into ½-inch cubes
2 egg yolks
2 Tb salad oil
½ c cold water

Mix the flour, sugar and butter in a mixing bowl on medium speed until the butter resembles small peas. Add the yolks, oil and water all at once and beat *only* until the dough begins to clump up.

Empty the bowl onto a floured counter and gently push into a mound. Using the heel of your hand, smear the flour and butter together by pushing against the mound and *away* from yourself. Work quickly, smearing all of the dough to approximately ⅛-inch thickness. Gather it up and reflour the counter.

Divide the dough in two and roll each half to approximately ⅛-inch thickness. Fit into two 9½-inch tart pans with removable bottoms. Cover with plastic wrap and place in the freezer until firm.

To partially bake, line the frozen tart shell with foil and fill with pie weights *(or rock salt, a much less expensive option).*

Bake in a preheated 400° oven until the edges begin to set, about 15 minutes.

Carefully remove the foil and return to the oven to bake until the edges are browning and the center has begun to dry out. *If they begin to puff up, do not prick the bottom if you are adding a runny filling—adding the filling will flatten out the bottoms.*

Makes two 9½-inch tart shells.

LEMON CHESS TART

1/4 c heavy cream

1/2 c butter

1/2 c corn meal

3 eggs

1 c sugar

zest and juice of **1** lemon

1 PÂTE BRISÉE Tart Shell,
9 1/2-inch, partially baked

powdered sugar & whipped cream, for garnish

Heat the cream and butter until the butter is melted. Add the cornmeal and allow it to sit for 5 minutes.

Beat the eggs and sugar until the mixture begins to thicken and become pale yellow.

Slowly pour the cornmeal mixture into the egg mixture, beating constantly.

Add the lemon juice and zest. Pour this mixture into the tart shell. Bake in a preheated 350° oven until the filling is golden and no longer shakes in the center, about 15 minutes.

Allow it to cool. Sprinkle with powdered sugar and serve with a dollop of slightly sweetened whipped cream.

Makes 1 tart.

Ann began making this tart in 1982 for the Shoalwater afternoon English high teas. Though they no longer serve high tea regularly, the Shoalwater frequently serves them to special groups.

For your own tea, accompany the tart with scones and jam, tea sandwiches and fresh strawberries. And a proper *cup of tea.*

ANN'S BREAD PUDDING

Amity Vineyards Late Harvest White Riesling
Comfort food like bread pudding requires comfort wine, if any. Myron's Late Harvest White Riesling is produced from Champoeg Vineyards Riesling grapes, yielding lush flavors without the cloying sweetness which would blow this dessert out of the water. A delicate and successful balance on its own.

This dessert has been the only constant on our dessert tray since we first opened the restaurant.

7 c day-old SHOALWATER FRENCH BREAD, torn into 1-inch pieces
½ c currants or raisins
3 eggs
4 egg yolks
½ c sugar
2 c half and half
1 c heavy cream
1 Tb Myers dark rum
½ tsp vanilla
CRÈME ANGLAISE, for a topping

Place bread pieces in an 8 by 8 inch baking dish. Sprinkle currants over the top.

Whisk together eggs, egg yolks and sugar in a medium mixing bowl. Add half and half, cream, rum and vanilla. Mix well.

Pour custard over bread. With the back of a spoon, press the bread down into the custard until all the bread is wet.

Cover the pan with foil, sealing the edges well. Set pan in a water bath coming halfway up the sides of the pan and bake in a preheated 350° oven until set, about 45 minutes. Cool.

Serve topped with CRÈME ANGLAISE.

Makes 6 to 8 servings.

Ann's Bread Pudding

Crème Anglaise

2 c half and half

3 egg yolks

¼ c sugar

1 Tb dark rum or Frangelico liqueur

¼ tsp vanilla

This basic dessert sauce appears several times throughout this book. Ann loves it because it is a quick and easy way to dress up so many desserts. Try it with apple pie (flavored with a little cinnamon schnapps!), poached pears (flavored with Poire Williams) or under a slice of rich, dark cake.

Heat the half and half in a sauce pan until just before it boils.

Beat the egg yolks and sugar in a mixing bowl until they become pale yellow and begin to thicken.

With the mixer on low, add the hot half and half in a slow stream.

Return the mixture to the sauce pan and cook over low heat, stirring constantly for several minutes, until the Crème Anglaise begins to thicken and coat a spoon. When it begins to thicken, remove it from the heat and add the rum and vanilla.

Crème Anglaise may be served warm or cold.

Makes 2 cups.

Woodward Canyon
Leonetti
L'École No. 41
Waterbrook
Seven Hills

Poached Oysters with Champagne, Brie & Saffron
L'École No. 41 Winery Washington Semillon

OR

Bleu Cheese Crisps
Seven Hills Winery Washington Sauvignon Blanc

Smoked Seafood Quenelles
Waterbrook Winery Reserve Chardonnay

OR

Paupiettes of Sole with Crab & Shrimp
Woodward Canyon Columbia Valley Chardonnay

Cranberry-Cabernet Sorbet

New York Pepper Steak
Leonetti Cellar Washington Cabernet Sauvignon

Rose Risotto
Woodward Canyon Washington Merlot (Charbonneau)

Hazelnut Stuffed Pears en Croûte
L'École No. 41 Winery Washington Chenin Blanc

WOODWARD CANYON
LEONETTI
L'ÉCOLE NO. 41
WATERBROOK
SEVEN HILLS

July 1, 1981. It takes a little over three hours to reach the Long Beach Peninsula from Seattle. As Ann and I took the Ocean Beaches exit off I-5 just south of Olympia and headed west on Highway 101, we noticed how uncrowded the four-lane road was, even during the summer, and how vast, green, and serene the landscape appeared. We became more and more relaxed as we got farther and farther away from the big city. When we took the Montesano cut-off which David Campiche, the inn's owner, had recommended as a time-saving way to skirt Aberdeen, the highway narrowed to a well-maintained two-lane road lined with huge evergreens, only occasionally interrupted by the scar of a recent clear cut. From time to time we could see a lonely farmhouse or a deer scampering into the woods. Occasionally a green highway sign pointed to small communities that could be reached by side roads—Artic, Pe Ell, Cosmopolis. After an hour, we passed through Raymond, a timber town with mountains of logs by the roadside, and South Bend, a fishing town with mountains of oyster shells by the Willapa River. For forty-five minutes along the lonely shores of Willapa Bay, we saw the Great Blue Heron scanning the tide flats for fish. After another fifteen minutes on some of the most tortuously winding roads in the state, we arrived at the blinking red light which marks the end of Highway 101 in the unincorporated beach community of Seaview.

It would have been easy to find the historic Shelburne Inn just a block or so north of the stop light, across the street from Sid's Supermarket, even if it had not been marked by a brass sign designating it as on the National Register of Historic Places. As we walked up the well worn wooden steps to the entrance, a smiling David Campiche came out to greet us, and as we entered the hotel, David's wife, Laurie Anderson, came from behind the massive antique altar table which still serves as the front desk to give us a warm welcome. The wood-lined lobby, with its big fireplace and antique furniture, felt homey and comfortable. When David and Laurie showed us the dining room, Ann and I exchanged incredulous "This is it!" looks. The dining room had the original 1896 tongue-in-groove siding and ceiling and was filled with solid old English tables and chairs, imported by David and Laurie as part of the antique business they run from the hotel.

Poached Oysters with Champagne, Brie & Saffron

1 c champagne
½ tsp saffron
½ tsp dried basil
1 pinch cayenne (or to taste)
1 qt small oysters, shucked
liquor from oysters
½ c sour cream
½ c heavy cream
8 oz Brie cheese, cut in 1-inch pieces with rind removed

Put champagne, saffron, basil and cayenne into a large sauce pan. Bring it to a simmer and add oysters and their liquor. Poach until they are plump and firm to the touch, about 3 minutes. Remove oysters to warm plates.

Over high heat, reduce the poaching liquid to ¼ cup.

Beat together the sour cream and cream. Stir into the poaching liquid and heat until it begins to bubble.

Add the Brie to the simmering sauce. Whisk until the cheese has melted and the sauce has thickened. Pour over the oysters and serve immediately.

Makes 6 servings.

Lowden Schoolhouse (L'École No. 41) Winery Washington Semillon
No bashful wine, this one. Lots of grassiness and oak, forward and full flavored. Reminds one of this winery's founder, Baker Ferguson, a retired Walla Walla banker and one of the more colorful characters in the industry. The sharp flavor of Brie cheese and the up-front mustiness of the saffron call for such a wine as this.

This is a rich and beautiful dish: even people who aren't great oyster fans love it.

BLEU CHEESE CRISPS

Seven Hills Winery
Washington Sauvignon Blanc
One of the newest additions to the Walla Walla winery scene, quickly establishing itself in the top rank. A delightful, clean, dry white wine with the varietal herbaceousness in just the right balance with the oak to refresh the palate at the beginning of a meal just as these savory "cookies" do.

You can make the dough for these ahead of time, then freeze or refrigerate. We recommend that you make a double batch—they disappear pretty quickly at our house.

½ lb bleu cheese
⅔ c butter, room temperature
¼ tsp cayenne
1 ⅓ c flour
½ c poppy seeds

Cream together the bleu cheese and butter until smooth.

Mix the cayenne with the flour and add it to the butter-cheese mixture. Blend well.

Divide the mixture in two, wrap each half in plastic and chill for 30 minutes.

Roll each ball of dough into a 1-inch thick cylinder, then roll each cylinder in the poppy seeds, coating them well.

Cut cylinders into ¼-inch slices. *They will slice better if slightly frozen first.* Place on a dry baking sheet and bake in a preheated 350° oven until golden brown, about 15 minutes.

Serve warm or at room temperature.

Makes 60 crisps.

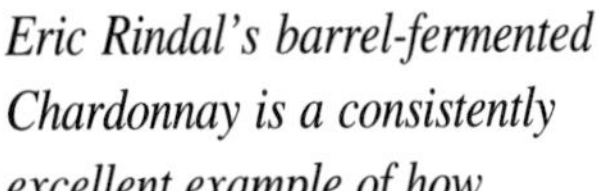

Smoked Seafood Quenelles

$\frac{1}{4}$ lb salmon, all bones, skin & membrane removed

$\frac{1}{4}$ lb smoked sturgeon

1 tsp white pepper

1 tsp dried parsley

1 tsp ground rosemary

1 egg white

1 c heavy cream, chilled

1 tsp salt

4 c simmering Shrimp Stock (or water)

1 $\frac{3}{4}$ c Rosemary & Leek Beurre Blanc

Waterbrook Winery
Reserve Chardonnay
Eric Rindal's barrel-fermented Chardonnay is a consistently excellent example of how important it is to select grapes carefully and then let them show their stuff. The distinct oakiness of this Chardonnay is a nice foil for the smokiness of the seafood. Not overwhelming in the mouth, it allows the delicate flavor of a quenelle to stand up on its own.

Purée the salmon and sturgeon in a food processor. Blend in the pepper, parsley and rosemary. Add the egg white and combine well. The purée must be very fine and well blended.

Place the purée in a bowl and set it into a larger bowl of ice. Cover it with plastic wrap and chill it for 1 hour.

With a wooden spoon, stir 3 tablespoons of the cream into the purée. Chill it for 15 minutes. Add another 3 tablespoons of the cream and beat it vigorously. Add the salt and chill for 5 to 10 minutes. Whip the remaining cream to form soft peaks and fold it into the purée.

The stock should be as hot as possible without bubbling—any motion will tear the quenelles apart. With 2 spoons dipped into hot water, mold the mousseline into small ovals and drop them into the simmering stock. When done, the quenelles will float to the surface.

Have plates ready with some Rosemary & Leek Beurre Blanc pooled on each one, and gently lay the quenelles on the sauce. Garnish with rosemary sprigs or poached leek designs.

Makes 6 servings (2 cups).

SMOKED SEAFOOD QUENELLES

ROSEMARY & LEEK BEURRE BLANC

In 1987, we began our series of monthly off-season wine dinners from October to May each year. These rather elaborate, and not inexpensive, dinners include fine Northwest wines matched with special dishes from our kitchen.

2 bunches leeks, white part only
3 Tb fresh rosemary, chopped (or **1 Tb** dried)
1 c grapefruit juice
¼ c white champagne vinegar
¼ c Irish whiskey
6 Tb white wine
6 Tb dry vermouth
2 c butter, chilled & cut into small bits

Thoroughly clean the leeks under running water. Slice the white part into thin slices. *You may save some of the greens for garnish. Cut designs from the greens and poach them before using to bring out a lovely green color.*

Combine all ingredients except the butter in a sauce pan. Bring to a boil, turn down the heat and simmer until it is reduced to 1 cup of liquid.

Purée the reduction and press it through a fine mesh strainer into a clean sauce pan.

When you're ready to serve, quickly heat the purée through. Remove from the heat and add the butter, bit by bit, stirring with a whisk. You can hold this sauce in a container set in warm water for a short while—*allowing it to cool or trying to reheat it once the butter is added will break the sauce.*

Makes 2 cups.

Paupiettes of Sole with Crab & Shrimp

2 Tb butter
3 oz mushrooms, sliced
2 scallions, sliced
1 stalk celery, diced
1 leek, white only, sliced
1 tsp dried tarragon
¾ lb Dungeness crab meat
¾ lb Oregon bay shrimp
1 c Parmesan cheese, grated
1 c Asiago cheese, grated
8 6-oz sole fillets
1 c white wine
2 c ASIAGO TARRAGON CREAM SAUCE

Woodward Canyon
Columbia Valley Chardonnay
Rick Small's wines in no way complement his surname. They are BIG: full-flavored, massively-structured, richly-crafted. Not much is left to the imagination with this ripe, powerful, forward Chardonnay. It requires fairly intensely flavored foods such as crab or shrimp—or lobster (unfortunately, not a Northwest product).

Melt the butter in a medium sauce pan. Sauté vegetables and tarragon until translucent. Drain off any excess liquid and toss with crab and shrimp. Let cool to room temperature and add the cheeses. Toss lightly to combine.

Firmly roll up the sole, cigar-style, around the stuffing.

Place fillets carefully in deep baking dish with the wine (adding more, if necessary, to come about a third of the way up the sides of the fish). Bake in a preheated 500° oven until sole is just firm, about 10 to 12 minutes.

To serve, put ¼ cup of ASIAGO TARRAGON CREAM SAUCE on each plate and top with the sole.

Grilled leeks make a great accompaniment. You can garnish with a julienne of leeks or scallions—don't be afraid to use the deep-green tops of the leeks for garnish. Poaching leek greens lightly heightens their color and makes them more pliable.

Makes 8 servings.

PAUPIETTES OF SOLE WITH CRAB & SHRIMP

SHOALWATER SHRIMP STOCK

A great way to always have stock on hand is to freeze it in ice cube trays. When frozen, transfer the cubes to a plastic container or zip-lock bags.

shells from **5 lb** of prawns
4 yellow onions, coarsely chopped
2 bunches leeks, coarsely chopped
1 c white vermouth
1 c Sherry
2 c white wine
5 qt water
¼ lb mushrooms
1 Tb dried chervil
1 Tb dried marjoram
1 Tb dried thyme
1 Tb dried rosemary
1 Tb whole black peppercorns
1 bay leaf

Put shells on a baking sheet in a preheated 350° oven until pink and dry, about 15 minutes.

Crush the shells in a food processor.

Put the crushed shells in a large stock pot with all the remaining ingredients and bring to a boil. Simmer for 30 minutes.

Strain, cool and refrigerate.

Makes 1 gallon.

Paupiettes of Sole with Crab & Shrimp

Asiago Tarragon Cream Sauce

1 ½ c fish stock
¾ c white wine
1 ½ c heavy cream
1 ½ tsp dried tarragon
¾ c Asiago cheese, grated
2 tsp flour
½ tsp kosher salt
¼ tsp white pepper

While it's true that the wine dinners have developed quite a following, we should explain that the majority of people who eat at the restaurant, both on and off season, select a much less involved dinner accompanied by a selection from a list of nearly five hundred wines from around the world.

Reduce the fish stock and wine in a sauce pan over high heat to half the original volume, about 1 cup.

In a second sauce pan, reduce the cream by half over medium heat, watching carefully that the cream does not boil over.

Combine the reductions into a single sauce pan and bring to a simmer. Add tarragon.

Toss the cheese with the flour until each piece is well-coated. Whisk the cheese into the simmering sauce and stir until smooth and thickened. Add salt and pepper. *You may substitute Parmesan or Romano cheese (freshly grated only) though the Asiago has a more pronounced flavor. Pre-grated, canned cheese will not melt properly.*

Keep warm over hot water until ready to use.

Makes 2 cups.

Cranberry-Cabernet Sorbet

4 c Cranberry Purée
2½ c 28° Sugar Syrup
¼ c cabernet or other red wine
1 tsp orange zest

Combine the ingredients and chill well. Freeze in an ice cream freezer according to the manufacturer's instructions.

For a sweeter sorbet, use Bogg's Cranberry Liqueur instead of red wine.

Makes 1 quart.

28° Sugar Syrup

5 c sugar
4¼ c water

Put the sugar and water in a sauce pan over medium heat, stirring to dissolve the sugar.

Remove the syrup from the heat as soon as it starts to boil.

The syrup can be kept for 2 to 3 weeks, covered in the refrigerator.

Makes 5 cups.

NEW YORK PEPPER STEAK

1 c black pepper, coarsely ground
6 8-oz New York steaks
¼ c clarified butter
½ c + 1 Tb butter
4 Tb green peppercorns
½ c shallots, minced
½ c brandy
3 Tb white wine vinegar
4 Tb soy sauce
1 c white wine
1 ¼ c veal demi-glace (**2½ c** SHOALWATER VEAL STOCK reduced to **1¼ c**)
½ c heavy cream

Place the pepper on a large plate, and press the steaks into it, coating all sides lightly.

Heat the clarified butter on medium-high heat and pan fry the steaks until done. Remove them to a warm platter and hold.

Pour off excess oil from the pan. Over high heat, add 1 tablespoon of the butter, green peppercorns and shallots. Sauté for 1 minute.

Deglaze the pans with brandy. *It will flame if you're cooking on gas—add it off the stove then return to the stove to flame it.* Add the vinegar, soy sauce and wine and reduce to ¾ cup. *Be patient—this will take 10 or more minutes.*

Add the demi-glace, bring to a boil and reduce to ½ cup.

Begin adding the cream a tablespoon at a time, reducing between additions, until the sauce becomes translucent and measures about ¾ cup.

continued...

Leonetti Cellar Washington Cabernet Sauvignon

Gary Figgins, the son of Italian immigrants to the Walla Walla Valley, transformed a winemaking hobby into one of the most respected winery names in the state. He concentrates on two varietals, Cabernet and Merlot, and year after year, produces quintessential examples of robust, beautifully layered wines from those varieties. If anything can stand up to Cheri's pepper steak, this is the wine that will do the trick.

NEW YORK PEPPER STEAK

...continued

Add the remaining ½ cup of butter, bit by bit, to finish and give shine to the sauce. Pour over the steaks and serve immediately.

Makes 6 servings.

The Shoalwater staff had a really stretching experience in 1990, when we designed and began to operate the first ocean front restaurant in southwest Washington, The Lightship. It is at the top of Nendels Inn in Long Beach, just a mile north of the Shelburne Inn, for families and wave watchers.

Rose Risotto

5 c red wine
4 c Shoalwater Veal Stock
3 Tb butter
2 Tb olive oil
2 Tb onion or shallot, finely chopped
1½ c Arborio rice
½ c Parmesan cheese
1 tsp salt
1 tsp pepper

Woodward Canyon Washington Merlot (Charbonneau)
As with his whites, Rick Small's Cabernet Sauvignon and his Merlot are not for the meek. Lots of fruit, lots of character—and with a few years of aging, lots of soft elegance. A lovely, rich dish paired with a flavorful, rich wine.

Put the wine in a sauce pan and reduce it to 2½ cups.

Add the veal stock to the wine and bring to a slow steady simmer.

In a large sauce pan, melt 2 tablespoons of the butter with the olive oil and sauté the onions until they are translucent.

Add the rice and stir until the grains of rice are coated. Add ½ cup of the wine-stock mixture and stir. *While adding the mixture to the rice, keep a boil high enough to be "lively," but low enough to evaporate the liquid slowly.* As the rice starts to dry out, add another ½ cup, stirring once. Repeat until all the wine-stock mixture is absorbed, about 20 minutes.

Have an extra cup of stock ready in case it's needed to finish cooking the rice. The rice is ready to serve when it is creamy with slightly *al dente* grains of rice.

Stir in the Parmesan and the remaining tablespoon of butter.

Makes 4 cups.

HAZELNUT STUFFED PEARS EN CROÛTE

2 Tb bread crumbs

¼ c hazelnuts, finely chopped

¼ c sugar

2 oz semi-sweet chocolate, finely chopped

2 Tb Frangelico liqueur

3 ripe Williams pears, peeled, halved & seeded leaving a 1 tablespoon-sized indentation

2 recipes PÂTÉ BRISÉE

1 egg yolk

1 recipe CRÈME ANGLAISE flavored with

2 Tb Frangelico liqueur instead of rum

Lowden Schoolhouse (L'École No. 41) Winery Washington Chenin Blanc
Baker Ferguson's penchant for a good pun results in Walla Voila!, this refreshing, fruity, slightly-sweet version of the Chenin Blanc, which will do very nicely with this not-too-sweet fruit dessert.

Blend the bread crumbs, nuts, sugar and chocolate in a food processor. Add the liqueur and pulse until it is moistened.

Pack this nut stuffing into the hollows in the pears.

Roll out ½ of the Pâté Brisée to ¼-inch thickness. Place one pear half, stuffing side down, near one edge of the dough. Cut out another section of dough large enough to completely cover the pear. Moisten the dough around the pear with a fingertip dipped in water, and then press the top layer onto the bottom. Using a fork or pastry wheel, press the layers together. With a paring knife, cut around the pear close to the markings, lift it gently and place it on a greased baking sheet. Repeat for the remaining 5 pear halves, using the remaining ½ of the Pâté Brisée for the last 3 pears. Set aside the remaining dough.

Cut leaves out of the left-over dough.

continued...

HAZELNUT STUFFED PEARS EN CROÛTE

...continued

Mix the egg yolk and 1 tablespoon water into an egg wash and brush each pear and each leaf. With the tip of a knife, draw the lines on the leaf.

Lay each leaf on a pear where it looks natural.

Bake them in a preheated 400° oven until they turn golden-brown, about 20 to 25 minutes. Remove and allow to cool slightly.

Serve warm with warm CRÈME ANGLAISE.

Makes 6 servings.

PONZI
ADELSHEIM
BETHEL HEIGHTS

CROUTONS OF ASPARAGUS & CRAB
Adelsheim Vineyard Washington Semillon

OR

SEAFOOD STUFFED MUSSELS
Bethel Heights Willamette Valley Chardonnay

SALMON WITH ROSE GERANIUM & GRAPEFRUIT BEURRE BLANC
Ponzi Vineyards Willamette Valley Chardonnay

OR

CRANBERRY BLUEBERRY SALMON
Ponzi Vineyards Reserve Pinot Noir

BONELESS LEG OF RABBIT WITH CHESTNUTS & APRICOTS
Bethel Heights Willamette Valley Pinot Noir

OR

GREEK-STYLE LEG OF LAMB
Adelsheim Vineyard Willamette Valley Pinot Noir

SALAD OF WILD GREENS WITH SHOALWATER HOUSE DRESSING

HARLEQUIN MOUSSE

PONZI
ADELSHEIM
BETHEL HEIGHTS

On our first visit to the Shelburne Inn, we were struck by a sense of deja-vue when David grabbed our bags and led us up the narrow steps to our cozy, carefully decorated room, especially when he showed us down the hall to the bathroom, complete with an oversized claw-footed bathtub. Later, when we joined David and Laurie in their small apartment just behind the front desk to discuss the possibility of our buying and operating the restaurant in the inn, we ate some of David's wonderful gravlax and bear sausage and Laurie's tasty homemade whole grain bread and shared an extraordinary bottle—or was it three? —of Oregon's Amity Vineyards 1978 Pinot Noir. A lasting friendship and a healthy business relationship began that weekend.

July 3, 1981. On the way back to Seattle we drove in silence for a long time, afraid to speak.

"What do you think?" Ann finally asked.

"I don't know," I answered. "It's perfect —but it's so far away from the city."

"The girls would love to live at the beach. I think we would too."

"Well, we could give it a try for awhile. At least, if it doesn't work out, nobody will even have to know. We could always go back to Seattle and tell people we've been on a long vacation."

October 5, 1981. Leading our first staff meeting with Ann and me were Chef Lorren Garlichs, a recent Culinary Institute of America graduate we had hired in Seattle, and Co-Managers Blaine and Cheri Walker, old friends from Seattle who had moved to Long Beach earlier to rear snails and escape the city rat race. The rest of the young crew had been interviewed and hired from the local community during the previous week.

I opened the meeting with a bold statement: "We're not giving up a good working and living situation in Seattle and moving down here just to operate a neighborhood Mom-and-Pop restaurant. I can't tell you when or how it will happen, but with your help we intend that this restaurant will make its mark."

Croutons of Asparagus & Crab

6 large slices Shoalwater French Bread
½ c olive oil
½ c lemon juice
1 c white vermouth
1½ c Shoalwater Shrimp Stock
3 Tb capers
2 shallots, minced
1½ c butter, chilled & cut into small bits
1½ lb fresh asparagus, trimmed evenly
1½ lb crab meat

Adelsheim Vineyards
Washington Semillon
For an Oregon winemaker, David Adelsheim produces a remarkably full range of varietal wines, including this excellent example of a grassy Semillon using Washington State grapes. This one is dry (but not overly so) and very giving in flavor to match up nicely with the refreshing chlorophyll aspect of the season's first asparagus and the sea-saltiness of Dungeness crab.

Fry the french bread slices in the olive oil until golden brown. Drain on paper towels and reserve.

Combine the lemon juice, vermouth, stock, capers and shallots in a sauce pan and reduce over medium heat until syrupy, to about ½ cup. Remove from heat and slowly incorporate the butter into the reduction, bit by bit, stirring constantly with a whisk. You may hold the sauce in a container set in warm–*not hot*–water.

Steam asparagus until tender, but still green and slightly crunchy. Arrange it on the toast.

Sauté or steam the crab meat just until warm, then lay it over the asparagus. Top with the warm sauce and serve immediately.

Makes 6 servings.

SEAFOOD STUFFED MUSSELS

Bethel Heights
Willamette Valley Chardonnay
Terry Casteel makes his wines with a perpetual student's touch, studiously extracting and balancing his flavors into very satisfying and clean examples of the subtle tastes available in the varietals with which he works. His medium-bodied Chardonnay displays all the nuances of the grape as it grows in Oregon soil. Cheri has produced here a seafood dish that plays well with the subtleties of this wine.

3 lb mussels, scrubbed & de-bearded
2 c white wine
7 strips bacon, diced
1½ onions, diced
1 stalk celery, diced
1½ green peppers, diced
1 Tb MAGIC DUST
2 tsp dried thyme
1 tsp dried oregano
8 oz shrimp meat
1½ c fish stock
5 oysters
5 green onions, sliced
½ c Parmesan cheese

Put the mussels in a covered sauce pan with the white wine and steam until opened. Cool and remove the top shell, leaving the mussel intact in the bottom shell. Reserve while you make the stuffing.

Sauté the bacon until nearly crisp, about 6 minutes on high heat. Add the onion, celery, green peppers, MAGIC DUST, thyme and oregano. Lower the heat to medium and continue to sauté until the vegetables are tender, about 5 more minutes.

Add the shrimp and sauté 2 minutes. Add the fish stock and simmer for 2 more minutes. Add the oysters and simmer for 1 minute.

Pour the mixture through a strainer, reserving the liquid. Purée the vegetables and seafood and return the purée to the pan with the reserved cooking liquid. Mix well and simmer until the stuffing becomes thicker or until all the liquid has reduced into the stuffing.

continued...

SEAFOOD STUFFED MUSSELS

...continued

Cool the mixture to room temperature and stir in the green onions and Parmesan cheese. Press a bit of the stuffing over each mussel in the shell and place on a baking sheet.

Bake in a preheated 500° oven for 7 minutes. Divide evenly among 6 plates. *You may wish to stabilize the mussels on a bed of rock salt.*

Makes 6 servings.

Ilwaco, our neighbor several miles to the south, has long been known as a sport salmon fishing center. The commercial fishermen who work out of that port also provide us with sturgeon, and Dungeness crab.

MAGIC DUST

- **1½ c** cayenne pepper
- **1 c** ground cumin
- **9 Tb** salt
- **4 Tb** paprika
- **4 Tb** garlic powder
- **1 Tb** thyme
- **1 Tb** dried basil
- **1 tsp** white pepper
- **1 tsp** black pepper
- **⅛ tsp** celery seed
- **8** bay leaves, crumbled

Mix together and you will have Shoalwater's Magic Dust.

Makes 4 cups.

Freeze it if you have more than you can use or give as gifts. To serve it with fish, add a bit of dill; if you serve it with meat, add a bit more bay.

Salmon with Rose Geranium & Grapefruit Beurre Blanc

Ponzi Vineyards
Reserve Pinot Noir
Left in the cellar for a few years, these elegant Pinot Noirs develop multiple layers of appealing flavor which exemplify the very reason the region has honed in on Pinot Noir as its favorite red-wine grape. I run the risk of losing wines through over-aging before I am willing to open them, but a ten-year-old Ponzi Pinot Noir can transport a dish—or an entire evening—to new heights while this salmon specialty provides a transport of its own.

1 large or **2** small grapefruit

10 large rose geranium leaves, finely chopped

1¼ c white wine

3 shallots, minced

2 Tb vinegar

1 c butter, chilled & cut into ½-inch pieces

4 7-oz salmon fillets

4 rose geranium leaves, for garnish

Peel off yellow part of the grapefruit skin and cut into thin julienne strips. Reserve for garnish. Juice the grapefruit—you should have about ¾ cup of juice.

Combine the chopped geranium leaves, grapefruit juice, ¼ cup of the wine, shallots and vinegar in a sauce pan and reduce over medium-high heat until it is slightly syrupy, to about ½ cup. Remove from heat and start incorporating the butter, bit by bit, whisking constantly until smooth. Hold over warm—*not hot*—water and serve as soon as possible.

Place salmon fillets in a baking dish with the remaining 1 cup of white wine. Bake in a preheated 500° oven until fish begins to flake, about 10 minutes. Drain slightly.

Pool some sauce onto each plate and set a fillet on each. Garnish with whole rose geranium leaves and reserved grapefruit strips.

Makes 4 servings.

SAUVIGNON BLANC

Cranberry Blueberry Salmon

¾ c dry white vermouth

1 ¼ c white wine

¾ c Cranberry Blueberry Mustard

¾ c butter, chilled & cut into small bits

6 6-oz salmon fillets

Combine vermouth and ¾ cup of the wine in a sauce pan. Bring to a boil and reduce over high heat to between ½ and ¼ cup.

Add Cranberry Blueberry Mustard and whisk thoroughly. Bring to a boil, whisk and remove from the heat. Whisk in the butter, a bit at a time, until the sauce has thickened and turned glossy. *If you need to hold the sauce, keep covered in a warm place such as over the stove or in a pan of warm water.*

Bake the salmon fillets with the remaining ½ cup of white wine in a preheated 500° oven until done, about 8 to 10 minutes.

To serve, pool ¼ cup of sauce on each plate and top with the salmon fillets. Garnish with a few port-poached berries.

This is great with salmon right off the grill or barbecue!

Makes 6 servings.

Cranberry Blueberry Salmon

Cranberry Blueberry Mustard

1 ½ c cranberries
1 ½ c blueberries
⅔ c raspberry vinegar
⅔ c sugar
¼ c Port
⅔ c dry mustard
1 c water
6 egg yolks

Cook cranberries, blueberries, vinegar, sugar and Port until the berries begin to pop, about 15 minutes. Remove from the heat and allow to cool.

Purée the mixture, strain through a medium sieve and set aside.

In a double boiler set over hot water, combine the mustard and water and beat until smooth. Add the egg yolks one at a time, whisking constantly until mixture thickens. Remove from the heat and stir in the berry purée.

This mustard will keep in the refrigerator for 2 weeks.

Makes 4 cups.

As a base for a butter sauce, this is unique. We use it as you would regular mustard, on sandwiches and burgers, and it can be mixed with mayonnaise or sour cream as a dip or salad dressing for fruit.

Boneless Leg of Rabbit with Chestnuts & Apricots

12 rabbit legs with thighs
¾ c dried apricots, chopped
½ c Scotch whisky, warmed
2 c cooked cous cous
4 c cooked basmati rice
10 oz canned chestnuts
6 Tb orange juice concentrate
2 Tb thyme
1 tsp salt
½ tsp pepper
½ c canola oil
2 c Whisky Orange Sauce, warmed
orange zest, for garnish

Bethel Heights Willamette Valley Pinot Noir
Rich, dark, soft and smoky flavors with hints of raspberries, cherries and red currants come to mind. The style at Bethel Heights tends to go to the medium-bodied with a definite gout du terroir, *or "taste of the earth" which marries beautifully with the grape's varietal aroma, particularly with a few years in the bottle—it offers an elegant finish to this rabbit preparation.*

Bone the rabbit thighs by cutting carefully around the thigh bone and pushing the meat up toward the leg. Carefully cut the bone away from the joint and remove it.

Soak the apricots in the Scotch for at least 1 hour.

Mix the cous cous, rice, chestnuts, orange juice concentrate, thyme, salt and pepper, tossing well to combine. Add the apricots and Scotch, mixing to distribute them evenly.

Stuff the legs and hold the opening closed by threading a toothpick through the skin.

Heat the oil in a sauté pan until hot and brown the legs on all sides. Roast in a preheated 400° oven until cooked through, about 20 to 30 minutes.

continued...

Boneless Leg of Rabbit

...continued

Remove from oven and slice the leg up to the leg joint. Pool some of the Whisky Orange Sauce on each of 6 plates and fan out the rabbit on top of the sauce. Garnish with bits of orange zest and sprigs of fresh thyme.

This recipe makes plenty of stuffing, so be generous when stuffing the legs. And don't forget to remove the toothpicks before slicing.

Makes 6 servings.

WHISKY ORANGE SAUCE

2 Tb clarified butter
1 onion, finely chopped
2 Tb balsamic vinegar
1 Tb dried thyme
6 oz orange juice concentrate
3 c chicken or rabbit stock
¼ c Scotch whisky
½ c heavy cream
4 Tb butter

Heat the clarified butter over medium heat in medium sauce pan. Add the onion and sauté until translucent.

Deglaze with the vinegar for a few seconds, then add the thyme, orange juice concentrate, stock and whisky. Bring up to a boil and reduce by half, to about 2½ cups.

Add the cream a bit at a time, never allowing the sauce to stop bubbling. Reduce to about 2 cups.

Add the butter, whisking continuously, until the sauce has thickened.

Makes 2 cups.

GREEK-STYLE LEG OF LAMB

Adelsheim Vineyards
Willamette Valley Pinot Noir
David Adelsheim's refined wines are a perfect complement to his wife Ginny's gorgeous labels, which display elegant painted portraits of friends and family. His Pinot Noirs are carefully crafted to extract as much flavor as the grape will yield and present it in lovely harmony with the moderate oak qualities which the wine picks up during the winemaking process. Lamb is a great meat to cook for Pinot Noir, as this recipe attests.

4 lb boneless leg of lamb (or **6 lb** bone-in)
8 c buttermilk
4 bay leaves
6 cloves
1 tsp juniper berries, crushed
½ tsp black peppercorns, crushed
3 tsp garlic, minced
3 Tb dried oregano
6 c cooked white rice
12 oz ham, diced
8 oz chicken, cooked & ground
12 oz feta cheese, crumbled
1 yellow onion, diced
2 Tb olive oil
¼ c parsley, chopped
4 hard-boiled eggs, sliced
2 c LEMON EGG SAUCE

If the lamb is bone-in, remove the bone from the leg completely. Lay the lamb flat between sheets of parchment to prevent tearing or splattering. Using a mallet, pound it to an even thickness. Put the meat in a pan large enough to hold it and the marinade in one layer.

Combine the buttermilk, bay leaves, cloves, juniper berries, peppercorns, garlic and 1 tablespoon of the oregano. Pour the marinade over the leg of lamb, cover and refrigerate overnight, turning occasionally.

In a mixing bowl, mix together the rice, ham, chicken, feta, onion, olive oil, parsley and the remaining 2 tablespoons of oregano.

continued...

GREEK-STYLE LEG OF LAMB

...continued

Remove the lamb from the marinade and pat dry.

Pat the stuffing evenly on the lamb and space the hard-boiled eggs lengthwise on top of the stuffing. Roll up the meat firmly and tie it securely at 1 inch intervals with butcher's twine.

Roast in a preheated 425° oven until done, about 1½ hours.

Remove it from the oven and allow it to set for about 15 minutes before slicing. Slice into 6 portions and serve on top of the LEMON EGG SAUCE. Pass any remaining sauce in a gravy boat.

Makes 6 servings.

GREEK-STYLE LEG OF LAMB

LEMON-EGG SAUCE

1 Tb flour

2 Tb butter, softened

2 c SHOALWATER VEAL STOCK

2 tsp dried oregano

¼ c fresh lemon juice

1 small onion, peeled & stuck with **2** cloves

¼ c Ouzo

2 egg yolks

Combine the flour and butter well. Set aside.

Combine the stock with the oregano, lemon juice and onion in a medium sauce pan. Bring to a boil and reduce it to 1 cup. Remove the onion.

Add the Ouzo and simmer for 10 more minutes.

Beat the egg yolks, then add ¼ cup of the hot liquid to the yolks in a thin stream, whisking constantly. Then add the yolk mixture back into the simmering liquid and keep stirring as the sauce begins to thicken.

Continue to stir while adding the flour-butter mix to the sauce in bits. When the sauce is further thickened, hold it over warm water until ready to serve.

Makes 2 cups.

SALAD OF WILD GREENS
WITH
SHOALWATER HOUSE DRESSING

½ c sour cream
6 Tb Dijon mustard
1 egg
1 egg yolk
2 ½ c salad oil
½ c red wine vinegar
1 tsp garlic, minced
½ tsp Worchestershire
salt & pepper, to taste

In a food processor or mixer, combine the sour cream, mustard and eggs until smooth and well blended.

With the mixer running, slowly add the oil in a thin stream. The mixture will thicken like mayonnaise as it emulsifies.

Add vinegar, garlic, Worchestershire, salt and pepper. Mix well—it should be very thick.

Use a strongly-flavored vinegar; a mild one will produce an oily tasting dressing. You can use Salalberry Vinegar or raspberry vinegar, or for a sweeter, nuttier taste, substitute balsamic vinegar for half of the red wine vinegar.

This dressing will hold for several weeks kept tightly covered in the refrigerator.

Makes 4 cups.

We are fortunate to have a large herb and edible flower garden at the restaurant and several growers raising unusual and usual lettuces and greens. We also have Southwest Washington's greatest forager, Veronica Williams, knocking at our back door with wild cresses, mints, goose tongue greens, miner's cabbage and salmonberry flowers—not to mention berries and mushrooms of all kinds. We make our salads every day according to our whim and what is on hand. You may have to rely on your market, but don't be trapped into paying a fortune for wild greens. If you aren't a forager yourself or just don't have anywhere to forage, select whatever greens are fresh and available and then add something whimsical: sprigs of mint or coriander or dill, a few pansies or nasturtiums. The dressing should do the rest...

Harlequin Mousse

6 eggs, separated
5 Tb sugar
8 oz bittersweet chocolate
½ c strong espresso coffee
2 Tb Kahlua (or coffee flavored liqueur)
pinch of salt
6 oz white chocolate
6 Tb butter
1 Tb instant espresso crystals

Beat 3 of the egg yolks with 3 tablespoons of the sugar until the yolks begin to turn pale yellow and thicken.

While the yolks are beating (it will take a while), melt the bittersweet chocolate with the espresso over low heat in a sauce pan or in a microwave. Stir until well mixed.

When the yolks have thickened, pour the hot chocolate mixture slowly into the yolks, mixing continuously. Stir in 1 tablespoon of the Kahlua.

In another bowl, whip 3 of the egg whites with the salt until they hold soft peaks.

Add one third of the whites into the chocolate, folding gently to incorporate. Fold in the remaining whites, being careful not to overmix, but making sure not to leave any white streaks in the mousse. Set aside.

Beat the remaining 3 egg yolks and the remaining 2 tablespoons of sugar until they become thick and pale. Add the espresso crystals and continue beating until the crystals dissolve.

Meanwhile, melt the white chocolate with the butter over low heat in a sauce pan or in a microwave. Stir until well mixed.

continued...

HARLEQUIN MOUSSE

...continued

Pour the hot melted white chocolate mixture slowly into the yolks, mixing continuously. Scrape the bowl and beat until thick. *It may separate—don't worry—keep beating and it will pull together.*

In a clean mixing bowl, beat the remaining 3 egg whites with a pinch of salt until they hold soft peaks. Fold the whites into the white chocolate mixture using the same technique as for the dark chocolate. Add the remaining tablespoon of Kahlua, folding gently.

Place each mousse in a 4-cup measure, then line up six serving glasses or bowls. Pour from each mousse simultaneously, filling each glass with half dark and half cappuccino at one time. Add a teaspoon of the dark chocolate mousse on top of the cappuccino mousse, or vice versa, as a decorative touch.

Makes 6 servings.

Hogue/Barnard Griffin
Arbor Crest
Ste. Chapelle

Poached Pepper-Lime Oysters
Arbor Crest Columbia Valley Sauvignon Blanc

OR

Asian Poached Oysters with Wild Greens & Shiitakes
Hogue Cellars Washington Fumé Blanc

Marinated Halibut with Minted Cream Sauce
Barnard Griffin Winery Columbia Valley Chardonnay

Rolled Pork Loin with Herbs & a Balsamic Mustard
Arbor Crest Columbia Valley Merlot

Grilled Duck Breast with Plum & Chanterelle Sauce
Hogue Cellars Reserve Cabernet Sauvignon

OR

Grilled Duck Breast with Juniper & Gin Sauce
Ste. Chapelle Vineyards Reserve Cabernet Sauvignon

Polish Apple Raisin Cake
Ste. Chapelle Vineyards Late Harvest Johannisberg Riesling

Hogue/ Barnard Griffin Arbor Crest Ste. Chapelle

The idea of doing a monthly series of special dinners focusing on the wines of the region occurred to us early in our tenure at The Shelburne. After all, we were perfectly located right "on the cusp"—roughly between the major vineyards of Washington and Oregon. We also had a strong personal connection with and interest in their wines. But it took five years of growth and development of our restaurant and wine cellar before we decided we were ready to do justice to such events.

Once we felt we were ready, however, it was relatively simple to set it all up. The easiest part was to call up our old winery friends from years past and invite them to spend a week-end at a lovely country inn near the beach enjoying good food and promoting their wines. Nobody declined. At first we concentrated on the best known and more established wineries so that we could offer a slightly different twist on the traditional winemaker's dinners we had seen advertised, most of which seemed to focus primarily on current releases. We wanted to be able to pour two or three vintages of at least one of the best wines from each winery in order to show off the development of the industry. By limiting the size of the dinners to about 40 people, we were able to convince the winemakers to shake loose a few reserve or library bottles which might otherwise not be readily available.

A little more challenging was getting the word out about our dinners. I still remember the first wine dinner we did in January 1987, when Rick Small brought all the wines he had ever made at Woodward Canyon Winery for sixteen of us to enjoy. Little by little, press releases and word of mouth succeeded in attracting a consistently good crowd for the dinners, which now have their own following.

The most challenging—and also one of the most enjoyable—part of organizing these events is always the planning of the menus for each dinner. Some of our regular diners might be surprised to discover that in our restaurant this is usually done by committee. Typically a few weeks before each event, I speak to each winemaker and find out what wines he or she is interested in spotlighting; we also discuss each wine's characteristics and the winemaker's food recommendations. If possible, we procure samples of at least several of the wines we have agreed on. I then talk about the wines with our kitchen and dining room managers at our regular weekly meeting. We discuss the wines in relation to the seasonal availability of seafood, meats and produce, with the goal of creating a new and interesting dish to complement each wine. This process for many would be doomed to failure but works remarkably well for us—and gets progressively easier with each passing year.

ASIAN POACHED OYSTERS

WITH
WILD GREENS & SHIITAKES

16 small oysters, shucked

1 c white wine

1 Tb soy sauce

1 tsp roasted sesame oil

8 oz bamboo shoots, drained & julienned

2 oz ginger root, peeled & julienned

½ lb fresh shiitake mushrooms, julienned

wild greens, enough for 4 small salads:
sorrel, mustard greens, watercress,
miner's cabbage, etc.

Poach the oysters lightly in the wine, soy sauce and sesame oil. Remove the oysters and keep them warm.

Add the bamboo shoots, ginger and mushrooms to the poaching liquid and reduce it to about ½ cup.

Arrange the oysters on the wild greens and pour the hot liquid over them. Serve immediately.

This dish may also be served chilled. To do so, chill the oysters and poaching liquid separately. When you are ready to serve, arrange the oysters on the bed of greens and pour the chilled sauce over them.

Makes 4 servings.

Hogue Cellars
Washington Fumé Blanc

The Fumé Blanc was successfully created as a marketing ploy for a then unpopular wine by Robert Mondavi in California years ago. Rob Griffin uses the alternative name for his Sauvignon Blanc, which aptly describes the smoky oakiness which he infuses into the traditional herbaceous character of this varietal. This smokiness pairs well with the full-bodied oyster taste-of-the-sea.

POACHED PEPPER-LIME OYSTERS

Arbor Crest Columbia Valley Sauvignon Blanc
Scott Harris makes one of the most consistently award-winning Sauvignon Blancs in Washington. This wine is full, forward and herbaceous, with a slightly floral quality which makes it very appealing. This redolent oyster preparation will delight even those who swear they can't stand oysters.

1 qt small oysters, shucked
liquor from oysters
½ c fresh lime juice (approximately 4 limes)
½ c champagne or white wine
2 Tb garlic, minced
¼ c olive oil
½ tsp salt
2 Tb coarse black pepper
3 bay leaves
2 red onions, very thinly sliced
½ c white wine vinegar
⅓ c sugar
1 tsp coarse cracked pepper

Heat the oyster liquor, lime juice and champagne in a large sauce pan until simmering. Add oysters and poach until firm, about 3 minutes. Transfer oysters to a medium bowl and reserve poaching liquid.

In a clean sauce pan, sauté the garlic in the olive oil until translucent. Add the salt, coarse ground pepper, bay leaves and 1 cup of the poaching liquid. Bring it to a boil and cook for 30 seconds. Cool to room temperature, then pour over oysters and refrigerate.

Combine onions with vinegar, sugar and cracked pepper. Allow to marinate 1 to 2 hours, or preferably, overnight.

To serve, make a bed of marinated onions on each plate and place oysters on top, or put a bed of the onions into a clean oyster shell and top with an oyster.

continued...

Poached Pepper-Lime Oysters

...continued

This dish is also excellent served hot. After poaching, remove the oysters to a warm plate and continue the recipe as written, except instead of cooling the sauce, finish it by adding 3 tablespoons of butter. Let simmer until the sauce thickens then pour over the warm oysters.

Makes 6 servings.

The original Pacific oysters from Willapa Bay fed the folks in San Francisco during the last century, and now our local Willapa Bay oysters feed the lucky diners at The Shoalwater.

MARINATED HALIBUT
WITH
MINTED CREAM SAUCE

Barnard Griffin Winery
Columbia Valley Chardonnay
Meanwhile, back at the homestead, Hogue Cellars' Rob Griffin and wife Deborah Barnard produce just a few cases of some very special Chardonnay, Fumé Blanc, and Cabernet Sauvignon—all go through malo-lactic fermentation and receive prolonged small barrel oak aging to produce rich, creamy wines. Not easily found, but worth seeking out. Certainly worth pairing with this marinated halibut.

12 sprigs fresh mint
12 sprigs fresh parsley
2 shallots, minced
½ tsp salt
¼ tsp pepper
½ c olive oil
juice of **1** lemon
½ c white wine
6 7-oz halibut fillets
1¾ c MINTED CREAM SAUCE
additional mint sprigs, for garnish

Combine the leaves from the mint and the parsley (discard stems) with the shallots, salt and pepper in a blender or food processor. With the motor running, slowly pour in the oil, then the lemon juice and the white wine.

Pour half the marinade in a dish large enough to hold the halibut in a single layer. Place the fillets on top, then pour the remaining marinade over the halibut. Refrigerate overnight or up to 24 hours.

This marinade is also great for prawns or scallops, or perhaps as a refreshing dressing for a cold rice or bulgur wheat salad.

Remove the halibut from the marinade. Grill it over a medium flame for 5 minutes, then flip and grill until it flakes, about 3 to 4 more minutes.

Pour ¼ cup of MINTED CREAM SAUCE on each plate, top with the halibut and garnish with mint sprigs.

Makes 6 servings.

Marinated Halibut

Minted Cream Sauce

12 sprigs fresh mint
1 sprig fresh tarragon, chopped
(or **1 Tb** dried)
1 sprig parsley, chopped
2 shallots, minced
¼ c white wine
¼ c white wine vinegar
⅓ c heavy cream
2 egg yolks, lightly beaten
1 c butter, chilled & cut into bits

Separate the mint leaves from the stems. Chop the leaves and set them aside.

Combine mint stems, tarragon, parsley, shallots, wine and vinegar in a medium sauce pan. Bring to a boil, then reduce it by half, to about ½ cup. Add cream and reduce by half again.

Strain into the top of a double boiler to remove the herbs and shallots.

Whisk in the egg yolks and then whisk in the butter, bit by bit, until the mixture thickens. Add the reserved chopped mint leaves.

Hold over hot water until ready to use.

Makes 1¾ cups.

Seaview, home of The Shoalwater, has been a summer haven for families from the Portland area since before the turn of the last century, and many of the lovely homes and cabins in our neighborhood which have been standing since then will probably still be here to enter the next century.

ROLLED PORK LOIN

WITH

HERBS & A BALSAMIC MUSTARD

Arbor Crest
Columbia Valley Merlot
Scott Harris' Merlots consistently exemplify Washington's growing conditions as ideal for that grape. He makes them in a richly-flavored, but supple style which will not overwhelm a lighter meat like veal or this rolled pork loin.

1 Tb each dried rosemary, thyme, oregano & parsley (double the amounts if you use fresh herbs)
3 shallots, finely chopped
3 green onions, finely chopped
3 cloves garlic, minced
3 Tb butter, melted
2 c bread crumbs
1 tsp salt
1 tsp pepper
2 lb boneless pork loin
3 Tb olive oil
½ c white wine
3 Tb BALSAMIC MUSTARD
1 c heavy cream
salt & white pepper, to taste

Mix together the herbs, shallots, green onions, garlic, butter, bread crumbs, salt and pepper. Set aside.

Trim the loin of all fat and silver skin. *Having a sharp boning knife and patience will make this next step easier. Go slowly and don't worry if you make a few holes—this takes practice. Or you can ask your butcher to flatten it for you.* Place the loin on the cutting surface pointing away from you (perpendicular to the edge of the counter). Starting at the center of the far end of the loin, slice down its length so it leaves a ¼ inch at the bottom intact. The loin is now splayed into two connected halves

continued...

ROLLED PORK LOIN

... continued

("butterflied") with the cut making a kind of "V" shape in the center of the loin. Lay your knife in this "V" so that the blade is flat, that is, parallel to the table. Now cut the left half in half—stopping before you cut all the way through—leaving a ¼-inch edge on the meat. Lay your knife in the center "V" again and cut the right half of the loin the same way. This should make the loin a large rectangle about ¼-inch thick.

Spread the stuffing on the pork in a thin layer. Roll it tightly, jellyroll fashion. Tie the roll in six places, evenly spaced. Cut between the ties to create six small roasts.

Heat the olive oil in a heavy pan and sear each roast on all sides. Lay them in a roasting pan and bake in a preheated 350° oven, turning them over once, until a meat thermometer registers 160°, about 20 to 25 minutes. Let roasts rest 10 minutes before slicing.

Deglaze the roasting pan with the white wine and reduce it to 2 tablespoons. Add the BALSAMIC MUSTARD and cream and reduce until it thickens. Season to taste with salt and pepper.

Divide the sauce between 6 plates and slice each roast and fan out slices on the sauce.

Makes 6 servings.

ROLLED PORK LOIN

BALSAMIC MUSTARD

1 c dark mustard seeds
1 ½ Tb Coleman's dry mustard
¼ c water
½ c red wine
1 ½ tsp honey
½ c balsamic vinegar
2 Tb apple cider vinegar
2 Tb sugar
4 tsp salt
2 cloves garlic, minced

Grind the mustard seeds in a blender or coffee grinder to the texture of ground pepper. Add the dry mustard and blend. Add the water and red wine and mix until blended.

Allow the mixture to stand for 1 to 4 hours, or overnight.

Pour the mixture into a food processor and add the remaining ingredients. Process until well blended.

Let the mustard stand at room temperature for 1 to 3 days to develop the flavor. Store in the refrigerator for a hotter mustard or at room temperature if you prefer a more mellow flavor. This mustard keeps indefinitely.

Makes 2 cups.

GRILLED DUCK BREAST
WITH
PLUM & CHANTERELLE SAUCE

1 ½ lb ripe plums,
pits removed & chopped
4 c chicken stock (or duck stock)
5 c Port
¼ c brandy
2 Tb Kirschwasser
2 Tb raspberry wine vinegar
¼ c heavy cream
¾ c butter, chilled
½ lb chanterelle mushrooms
8 duck breasts

Hogue Cellars Reserve Cabernet Sauvignon
Hogue winemaker Rob Griffin competes with his own Barnard Griffin Cabernet Sauvignon, making a dense, intense, and elegant reserve Cabernet at Hogue: both are winners. The bouquet of chocolate, tobacco and smoke shows through the black currant aroma of the Cabernet grape in a gorgeous wine for dark-meat fowl such as duck breast, grilled as Cheri suggests here.

If using whole ducks, remove the breasts and leg-thigh pieces. Make stock with the carcasses. Save the legs for another meal, or use them in this preparation. They will take longer to cook, however, so they should be grilled partway and then finished in the oven. They are done when the juices run clear when you pierce the leg.

Combine plums and stock in a sauce pan, bring to a boil and simmer until the skins pop. Strain into a second sauce pan, forcing the fruit through the strainer to purée it.

Add the Port, Brandy, Kirschwasser and vinegar to the purée. Bring it to a boil and simmer until it is reduced by half. Add the cream and simmer until the sauce begins to thicken and clarify. Add ½ cup of the butter, bit by bit, whisking continuously until thickened. Hold over warm water until ready to use.

Melt the remaining 4 tablespoons of butter in a sauté pan. Add the mushrooms and sauté until they absorb the butter. Pour the plum sauce into the pan and toss

continued...

Grilled Duck Breast
with
Plum & Chanterelle Sauce

...continued

with the mushrooms until they are coated. Keep the sauce warm over hot water while you cook the duck.

Grill the duck breasts over a medium flame. They should be resilient to the touch and still slightly pink when done.

To serve, slice the duck breasts thin, ladle sauce onto serving plates and fan the duck across the sauce.

Makes 8 servings.

Grilled Duck Breast
with
Juniper & Gin Sauce

5 Tb butter, chilled & cut into bits
3 leeks, white part only, chopped
1 clove garlic, minced
½ c gin
juice of **1** lemon
1 c orange juice concentrate
(reduce 4 c to 1 c if using fresh juice)
4 c chicken stock
(or duck stock if available)
¼ c heavy cream
6 boneless duck breasts
6 Tb B & B Butter

Ste. Chapelle Vineyards Reserve Cabernet Sauvignon
Idaho's Ste. Chapelle Vineyards has become one of the largest-producing wineries in the entire region. More known for their ubiquitous white and sparkling wines, they are quietly building up an impressive array of reserve Cabernet bottlings which are released only when well-aged and in great shape. The intensity and balance of these wines will do wonders for Cheri's grilled duck breast with juniper and gin.

Melt 2 tablespoons of the butter in a sauce pan over medium heat. Add the leeks and garlic and sauté until translucent.

Add the gin (off the stove if cooking with gas) to deglaze the pan. Continue cooking to reduce liquid to ¼ cup. Add the lemon juice and orange juice concentrate and cook, bubbling, until reduced to 1 cup. Add the stock, bring to a slow boil and reduce to 2 cups.

While the sauce boils, add the cream, a bit at a time, letting the sauce thicken and lose its cloudiness between additions.

Stir in the remaining 3 tablespoons of chilled butter to finish the sauce. Strain out the leeks and garlic and keep the sauce warm while you cook the duck.

Grill the duck breasts over a medium flame. They should be resilient to the touch and still slightly pink when done.

continued...

Grilled Duck Breast

... continued

The leg-thigh pieces of the duck can also be used. However, they take much longer to cook. At the Shoalwater, we grill the legs until they're nicely browned, then pop them into a hot oven to finish cooking. Another way to serve them is a la Francaise *by serving the breasts first, then the legs as tasty post-entrée nibble. Mmmmmmmmm.*

To serve, slice the duck breasts thin, pool some of the citrus sauce on each plate and fan the duck across the sauce. Place 1 tablespoon of the B & B Butter on top of the duck and serve it as the butter melts.

For chicken stock use any recipe from a standard cookbook. To make a duck stock simply substitute duck for the chicken bones.

Makes 6 servings.

B & B Butter

1 c butter, softened
½ tsp white pepper
½ tsp black pepper
1 Tb juniper berries, ground
2 Tb B & B liqueur
¼ tsp lemon zest

The butter rosettes can be frozen and held until used. Make sure to defrost in the refrigerator for an hour before using.

Beat the butter in an electric mixer until it becomes creamy and smooth. Add the peppers, juniper berries, liqueur and lemon zest and mix well.

Fill a pastry bag fitted with a star tip—*you might have to bend the prongs out a bit so the butter doesn't get stuck*—and pipe the butter into rosettes or designs of your choice. Refrigerate until firm.

Makes 1 cup.

Polish Apple Raisin Cake

1½ c butter
2 c sugar
4 eggs
2 c flour
2 tsp cinnamon
1 tsp baking soda
3 c apples, grated
1½ c raisins
1½ c walnuts, coarsely chopped
½ c brown sugar, packed

Ste. Chapelle Vineyards Late Harvest Johannisberg Riesling
The Northwest's wine reputation began with the discovery of the region's ability to produce great Rieslings, ranging from very dry to very sweet. This example from Idaho's Ste. Chapelle is representative of a moderately-sweet wine with rich flavors of honey and peaches, one which I enjoy with Ann's delicious apple raisin cake.

Soften 1 cup of the butter and beat it with the sugar until the mixture is light and pale.

Add the eggs one at a time and mix until incorporated. Beat at medium speed for 3 minutes.

Add the flour, cinnamon and baking soda; beat 3 more minutes.

Reserve 1 cup of the apple, ¾ cup of the raisins and ¾ cup of the nuts. Fold the remaining fruits and nuts into the batter.

Grease and flour a 10-inch springform pan. Pour the batter into the pan and smooth the top. Bake in a preheated 350° oven until a toothpick inserted into the middle comes out clean, about 1½ hours.

Allow the cake to cool while you make the topping.

Melt the remaining ½ cup of butter with the brown sugar. Bring to a boil. Reduce heat and add the reserved apples, raisins and nuts. Cook slowly until the raisins plump and the sauce begins to thicken.

Pour the topping over the cake and allow it to cool. Remove the cake from the pan and serve.

Makes 12 generous slices.

Sokol Blosser
Knudsen Erath
Rex Hill

Smoked Trout Flan
Sokol Blosser Winery Willamette Valley White Riesling

OR

Innkeeper's Mussel Chowder
Rex Hill Vineyards Willamette Valley Chardonnay

Marinated Quail with Sauce Romesco
Knudsen Erath Vintage Select Pinot Noir

Veal Loin in a Cherry & Pinot Noir Sauce
Rex Hill Maresh Vineyard Pinot Noir

Minted Lamb Sausage Salad
Sokol Blosser Vineyards Redland Pinot Noir

Honey Walnut Tart

OR

Portuguese Port Flan

SOKOL BLOSSER
KNUDSEN ERATH
REX HILL

There is no question that the Shoalwater Wine Dinners are complicated to produce, considering that we are usually making each dish for the first time in this quantity. We get to learn as we go, and that makes it very exciting, and sometimes nerve-wracking. On a number of occasions, when we were sure we had failed miserably with a particular dish, the diners have seen it quite differently and remark on how good that item was.

To keep life interesting at all times at the restaurant, we have made it a point to change our menus every few weeks to take advantage of seasonal offerings as well as to challenge the creativity of our chefs. I still remember vividly a time while I worked at The Other Place in Seattle when we had become complacent because of our growing national reputation: We thought we could do no wrong. I began to notice a marked increase in the number of verbal or written complaints regarding the food or the service and realized we had stagnated in the midst of our own success. Having become aware of the problem, we were able to reverse it. I vowed then always to be on the lookout for the syndrome.

The winemaker's dinner series has provided us with a natural opportunity to stretch and learn. It also has allowed us to experiment with a captive audience, free from the constant concern chefs have about the wisdom of putting something unusual on the menu. We have discovered some wonderful items which have made their way onto our regular menus or turn up as daily specials when limited-supply items come into the kitchen. They have provided our veteran kitchen staff with countless new learning experiences and a great forum to train newer cooks or apprentices about techniques or preparations which they would not ordinarily come across on a daily basis in any restaurant.

It is amusing to look back at the original, and very simple, menu we opened with in 1981 and compare it to the kind of items we serve at such special events or even those which are found on our regular menu today. It is a tribute both to the development of our staff and to the increased sophistication of our clientele.

The greatest compliment that can be paid the chef and/or owner of a restaurant comes when a guest puts down the menu and says: "Just do dinner." In essence, we are paid this compliment each month by 25-40 people when they sign up for one of our wine dinners, having no idea what we will do. We are certainly honored and do not take this trust lightly. However, when all is said and done, we do have a helluva good time making the food and wines of the Pacific Northwest look and taste so good!

SMOKED TROUT FLAN

1 c heavy cream

1 c half and half

2 oz fresh morel mushrooms, chopped (or ½ **oz** dried, soaked in hot water for 1 hour)

1 Tb orange zest

1 Tb lemon zest

2 Tb apple brandy

½ tsp salt

¼ tsp white pepper

½ lb flaked smoked trout

2 Tb fresh chives, chopped

9 egg yolks

Put cream, half and half, morels, zests and brandy into a sauce pan. Simmer the mixture for 15 minutes. Remove from heat, add the salt, pepper, trout and chives and set the mixture aside.

Lightly beat the egg yolks in a mixer. With the mixer running on low, add the hot cream mixture in a slow stream. Mix just until combined.

Pour into six 6-ounce custard cups. Set them in a large pan and fill it with enough hot water to come halfway up the sides of the custard cups.

Bake in a preheated 350° oven until a knife inserted in the middle comes out clean, between 45 and 60 minutes. Allow them to cool, then refrigerate overnight.

To unmold, let the custard sit at room temperature until it warms slightly. Briefly dip each cup in hot water and loosen the flan by running a narrow-bladed knife around the edge of the cup. Invert directly onto plates.

This is both beautiful and flavorful served on a bed of SPINACH AND SORREL CHIFFONADE SALAD WITH RIESLING, SHALLOT & APPLE DRESSING.

Makes 6 servings.

Sokol Blosser Winery
Willamette Valley
White Riesling

Oregon's Rieslings tend to be very dry, but display a lovely floral fruity varietal quality. Bill Blosser makes a lovely dry one as an excellent example of how well the grape does in Oregon. Its delicate flavors work wonders with Cheri's light fish custard.

Smoked Trout Flan

Spinach & Sorrel Chiffonade Salad with Riesling, Shallot & Apple Dressing

The Chiffonade:

- **12** medium French sorrel leaves
- **12** medium spinach leaves
- **½ c** Riesling, Shallot & Apple Dressing

Rinse and remove stems and ribs from the sorrel and spinach leaves. Pat the leaves dry and stack them. Carefully roll the stack like a cigar and slice across the roll, no wider than ⅛ inch, to create thin strips (chiffonade).

Have dressing warm, but not boiling. Toss the chiffonade with the warm dressing, divide evenly between 6 plates and serve immediately.

Makes 6 servings.

Just two blocks from the beach, The Shelburne Inn and The Shoalwater Restaurant are a cozy contrast to a winter storm or a perfect finish to a day of beach combing.

INNKEEPER'S MUSSEL CHOWDER

Rex Hill Vineyards Willamette Valley Chardonnay
Paul Hart's affection for the great French Burgundies is evident in the quality of the classic Chardonnays and Pinot Noirs he releases at Rex Hill. Made well and made to last, the winery's Chardonnays are full-flavored, fruity, oaky and buttery but well-balanced to make it for the long haul. A nice match for our all time favorite chowder.

5 lb Penn Cove or other Northwest mussels
1 c water (or white wine)
2 medium potatoes, peeled & diced
1 large yellow onion, diced
1 stalk celery, diced
2 Tb butter
1 28-oz can tomato sauce
2 c heavy cream
1½ tsp dried basil
2 tsp curry powder
salt & pepper, to taste

Steam mussels in a covered pot with the water until they open. Shuck them, reserving both the cooking liquid and the mussel meats.

Parboil the potatoes until halfway done. Drain.

Sauté the onion and celery in the butter until the onions turn translucent. Add the potatoes and toss to coat with butter.

Over medium heat, add the tomato sauce, cream and reserved mussel liquid, stirring well. Add basil, curry, salt and pepper. Simmer 35 minutes, stirring frequently from the bottom to prevent scorching.

Add mussels. Heat through and serve.

When you make this chowder, be sure to taste and correct the seasoning: Mussels vary greatly in saltiness.

Makes 8 cups.

MARINATED QUAIL WITH SAUCE ROMESCO

3 Tb olive oil
6 quail
1 medium onion, chopped
6 cloves garlic, peeled
1 Tb shallots, minced
2 carrots, sliced 1/8-inch thick
1 stalk celery with leaves, chopped
2 bay leaves
2 sprigs parsley
1 tsp thyme
1/2 tsp salt
10 peppercorns
pinch saffron
3/8 c red wine vinegar
3/8 c chicken stock
1 1/2 c white wine
1 1/2 c SAUCE ROMESCO
lemon slices or zest, for garnish

Heat the olive oil in a medium sauce pan. Sauté the quail until well browned. Remove the quail and set them aside.

In the same oil, sauté the onion, garlic, shallots and carrot until wilted. Add the celery, herbs, salt, peppercorns and saffron.

Stir in the vinegar, stock and wine. Add the quail, cover and simmer for 45 minutes.

Remove quail. Bring to a boil and reduce marinade an additional 3 minutes and pour over quail. Cover and refrigerate for 3 to 4 days, turning occasionally.

Serve the quail at room temperature with SAUCE ROMESCO, garnished with lemon slices or zest.

Makes 3 to 6 servings.

Knudsen-Erath Vintage Select Pinot Noir

Dick Erath's best effort every vintage goes into his Vintage Select label, which in good years yields clean, delicious, long-lasting Pinot Noirs. Dick is a big, friendly, down-home, but quality-driven type of guy—and so are his wines. This is one of the reasons we enjoy the chance to match a fowl such as quail to this fine Pinot.

MARINATED QUAIL

SAUCE ROMESCO

Down the block and around the corner from the restaurant, stands the historic Colley House one of Seaview's little jewels of Victorian architecture.

4 roma tomatoes

3 dried Ancho chiles, soaked in warm water for 1 hour, seeded & minced

10 cloves garlic, minced (about 2 Tb)

½ c almonds, blanched & roasted

½ c hazelnuts, roasted

2 sprigs parsley, leaves only, chopped

3 slices SHOALWATER FRENCH BREAD, fried in **4 Tb** olive oil

2 Tb red wine vinegar

4 Tb olive oil

¾ c chicken stock

½ tsp cayenne pepper

1 tsp salt

Bake tomatoes for 10 minutes in a preheated 350° oven. Remove and cool.

In a food processor, make a thick paste of the chiles and garlic. Blend in the nuts, parsley and fried bread.

Peel, seed and chop the tomatoes. Blend into the *paste*.

Add vinegar, oil, chicken stock, cayenne and salt. The mixture should resemble a soft peanut butter.

Makes 3 cups.

Veal Loin in a Cherry & Pinot Noir Sauce

½ c clarified butter

3 lb veal loin, trimmed & cut into 6 8-oz roasts

flour, for dusting

2 c Cherry & Horseradish Hollandaise

2 c Cherry Pinot Noir Sauce

3 c Popped Wild Rice

Heat clarified butter in a sauce pan large enough to hold the veal roasts. Dust the veal lightly with flour, then brown them in the butter on all sides.

Place the veal in a roasting pan fitted with a rack and cook in a preheated 500° oven until a meat thermometer registers 120°, about 15 to 20 minutes. Remove the pan from the oven and let the meat rest for about 5 minutes.

Meanwhile, pool about ¼ cup of each Cherry Sauce side by side on a warmed plate, and run a line of the Popped Wild Rice through the center of each sauce.

Slice the veal roasts into medallions and place on top of the sauce and rice. Pass any extra sauce in a sauce boat.

Makes 6 servings.

Rex Hill Maresh Vineyard Pinot Noir

Paul Hart releases a series of vineyard-designated Pinot Noirs each year, believing as he does in allowing the flavor of the soil at each site to show through the wine. Maresh (pronounced "marsh") Vineyard is one of Oregon's best, and this wine yields consistently intense, complex wines which only develop even more beautifully with a few years in the bottle. This great sauce needs a great wine like this one!

VEAL LOIN

CHERRY PINOT NOIR SAUCE

½ c dried cherries

2 c veal demi-glace (**4 c** SHOALWATER VEAL STOCK reduced to 2 c)

1 c Madeira

1 c Pinot Noir

½ c heavy cream

½ c butter, chilled & cut into bits

Combine cherries, demi-glace, Madeira and Pinot Noir in a sauce pan and reduce by almost half, to about 2 cups.

Whisking continuously, add the cream to the simmering sauce, a bit at a time, until the sauce becomes translucent and the volume is about 1½ cups.

Still whisking, add the butter, a bit at a time, to finish and add a glisten to the sauce.

Makes 2 cups.

Veal Loin

Shoalwater Veal Stock

10 lb veal bones

1 carrot, unpeeled & roughly chopped

1 large yellow onion,
with skin & roughly chopped

2 stalks celery, roughly chopped

3 roma tomatoes, quartered

3 c white wine

3 c red wine

1 ½ c Madeira

2 sprigs parsley

1 Tb dried marjoram

1 Tb dried thyme

1 Tb dried rosemary

2 Tb black peppercorns

2 bay leaves

water to cover

For some of our recipes, we prefer to pre-reduce the stock by half, called a "demi-glace" or simply a "demi." Using a demi makes a reduction happen faster and there is less volume to store. Demi-glace can be frozen in ice cube trays and stored in zip-lock bags for future use.

Put bones in a preheated 500° oven until they are well browned, about 45 minutes. Remove from oven.

Spread the carrot, onion, celery and tomatoes over the bones and return the pan to the oven to brown the vegetable skins, about 20 more minutes.

Put the bones and vegetables into a large stock pot—*they should fill the pot no more than two thirds of the way to the top.* Add all the remaining ingredients, using enough water to cover. Bring to a full boil, turn down the heat and simmer for 5 hours. *If the level of water drops below the level of the bones, add hot water to cover again.*

Strain into clean containers and cool, then refrigerate. Remove the fat from the surface once it has solidified.

Makes 1 gallon.

VEAL LOIN

CHERRY & HORSERADISH HOLLANDAISE

2 c cherry wine (or Pinot Noir)

2 shallots, minced

¼ c dried Bing cherries

1 c butter

5 egg yolks

1 Tb prepared horseradish

2 Tb heavy cream

½ tsp salt

Combine the wine, shallots and cherries in a sauce pan and reduce to a glaze, about ¼ cup.

Melt the butter until hot but not browned. Put the egg yolks in a food processor fitted with the metal blade. With the processor running, pour in the hot butter in a slow stream.

Add the horseradish and wine reduction and process well to combine and chop the cherries.

Add the cream and salt and pulse just to combine. Use the sauce immediately.

Makes 2 cups.

VEAL LOIN

POPPED WILD RICE

3 c peanut or canola oil
2 c wild rice

A deep-fryer with a basket will work very nicely for this as long as the rice cannot get through the mesh of the basket. Otherwise a large strainer, a metal bowl and sauce pan will work just fine.

Set a large strainer over a metal bowl.

Heat the oil in a large sauce pan on the stove until it just starts smoking—about 380° on a deep-fry thermometer.

Toss in 1 grain of rice to test the heat—it should sink to the bottom and then puff up to float on top of the oil within 2 seconds. If it takes longer, heat the oil a bit more and keep testing.

When the oil is hot enough, pour in the rice all at once and gently shake the pan until the bubbling stops and the rice has all risen to the top of the oil.

Drain immediately *and carefully* through the strainer. Shake the strainer slightly to drain off any excess oil.

You may re-strain the oil through cheesecloth and heat it with a few quarter-sized slices of ginger root. This freshens the oil so that it can be used again for deep-frying. Cool the oil thoroughly before transferring to a storage container.

Makes 6 cups.

This rice has a crunchy, nutty flavor that lends itself well to poultry. It can also be used as a garnish on soups or thrown into pancake or waffle batter to make an unusual starch accompaniment for appetizers or entrées.

MINTED LAMB SAUSAGE SALAD

Sokol Blosser
Redland Pinot Noir
The Redland label at Sokol-Blossser has been recently developed as a hybrid of two estate vineyards and intended to showcase the winery's top-of-the-line wines each vintage. This Pinot Noir has enough richness and fullness to stand up very nicely to Cheri's lamb sausage, which does equally well at a fancy dinner or at an ocean front picnic.

Sausages:

1 lb ground lamb
½ c currants
½ c fresh mint leaves, minced (**10 sprigs**)
1 Tb pinenuts
1 tsp garlic, minced
1 tsp fennel seed, ground
¼ tsp cinnamon
¼ tsp cardamom
¼ tsp mace
2 Tb Port
2 Tb Pinot Noir
1 Tb brandy

Combine all ingredients and mix well. Refrigerate overnight.

Form the sausage into small patties about the size of a silver dollar.

To serve, grill the patties about 1 minute on each side.

Makes about 24 small patties.

Minted Lamb Sausage Salad

6 c mixed salad greens, such as romaine, batavian and leaf lettuces, small amounts of mint, oregano, cornsalad, rocket, sorrel, watercress and lambs quarter

3/4 c Salalberry Vinaigrette

6-8 oz Quillisascut feta cheese (or other fresh feta cheese)

12 grilled Minted Lamb Sausages

Toss salad greens with the Salalberry Vinaigrette. Portion onto 6 plates.

Top each salad with 1 to 1½-ounces of cheese and 2 each of the warm grilled sausages.

Makes 6 servings.

Minted Lamb Sausage Salad

Salalberry Vinaigrette

¼ c Salalberry Vinegar
½ tsp garlic, minced
1 ½ tsp honey
2 tsp fresh oregano, finely chopped
½ c olive oil
¼ c peanut oil
½ tsp salt
½ tsp pepper

Combine the vinegar, garlic, honey and oregano in a bowl with a whisk.

Combine the oils and pour them into the vinegar mixture in slow stream, whisking constantly.

Add the salt and pepper.

Makes 1 cup.

Minted Lamb Sausage Salad

Salalberry Vinegar

2 lb salalberries

$\frac{1}{4}$ c sugar

1 stick cinnamon

1 $\frac{1}{2}$ gal white wine vinegar

Put all the ingredients in a stockpot and heat to just below a simmer.

Cook uncovered for 30 minutes, pushing the berries down occasionally. Cool to room temperature, then cover.

Allow the liquid to sit with the berries at room temperature for 4 to 6 weeks.

Strain through a cheesecloth. Pour into bottles—there are beautiful gift bottles available—and store in your pantry for gifts.

Makes 1$\frac{1}{2}$ gallons.

This is an earthy, authoritative vinegar that smells like a Northwest forest. We make a vinaigrette for our dinner salads, which is distinctively flavored. However, we also use this vinegar to balance sauces that are too sweet or too rich with cream or butter. Also good in marinades, this vinegar adds zest to grilled meats or mushrooms.

HONEY WALNUT TART

1 ½ c sugar

½ c water

¾ c butter, cut into small bits

1 c milk

⅓ c honey

3 c walnuts, coarsely chopped

1 9 ½-inch PÂTE BRISÉE tart shell, partially baked

2 oz semisweet chocolate

whipped cream, for serving

Boil the sugar and water in a medium sauce pan over high heat until the color begins to turn amber. Swirl the pan occasionally until the syrup becomes a rich caramel color.

Remove the pan from the heat and add the butter and milk all at once. Return to the heat and bring back to a boil. Reduce the heat to low and simmer for 15 minutes.

Remove from the heat and stir in the honey and the nuts. Cool slightly.

Pour the mixture into the tart shell and bake in a preheated 400° oven for 15 minutes. Remove and cool to room temperature. *The filling will develop "holes."*

Melt the chocolate in a double boiler. Drizzle the chocolate over the cooled tart, making a random squiggly pattern.

Chill the tart and serve with unsweetened whipped cream. *This is a rich concoction—you needn't serve a big slice!*

Makes 8 to 12 servings.

PORTUGUESE PORT FLAN

3 c sugar
1 orange
1 lemon
2 c heavy cream
2 c half and half
12 egg yolks
¼ c Port

These flans are wonderful with a glass of good Port! Try Whidbey's Port from Washington.

Heat 2 cups of the sugar in a large sauce pan over high heat. Stir constantly, breaking up lumps of sugar as they form. *Work quickly once the sugar begins to liquify—it will burn easily.* Cook only until it turns a rich golden color. *Do not overcook—it will continue to cook once removed from the heat.*

Pour about 2 tablespoons of the caramelized sugar into each of 10 custard cups, swirling each cup to coat the sides evenly, pouring any excess into the next cup. Leave about 1 tablespoon of caramel in the pan.

Peel the outer colored layers of the lemon and orange and reserve the fruit flesh (the sections) for another use.

Add the peels, cream, half and half and the remaining 1 cup of sugar to the pan with the reserved caramel. Bring it to a boil, stirring constantly, and then allow it to barely simmer for 15 minutes.

Remove the cream mixture from the heat. Strain out the peels.

Put the yolks in the bowl of an electric mixer and mix lightly. With the mixer on low, add the hot cream mixture to the yolks in a steady stream, mixing only until well blended. Add the Port and mix briefly.

Divide the mixture among the 10 custard cups.

continued...

PORTUGUESE PORT FLAN

...continued

Place the cups in a large roasting pan and fill the pan with enough water to come halfway up the sides of the custard cups. Bake in a preheated 350° oven until a knife inserted in the middle comes out clean, about 45 minutes.

Allow them to cool in the water bath to room temperature, then take them out of the water. Chill completely.

To serve, run a narrow-bladed knife around the edge of the cup and invert each over a plate. Scrape the excess caramel over the top.

Makes 10 servings.

Paul Thomas
Salmon Bay
Quilceda Creek

Smoked Salmon-Whitefish Sausage
Salmon Bay Winery Oyster Shell White

OR

Smoked Salmon Mousse
Paul Thomas Washington Chardonnay

French Bread

Orange-Saffron-Tomato Cod
Salmon Bay Winery Washington Chardonnay

OR

Wild Mushroom-Sake Sturgeon
Paul Thomas Reserve Chardonnay

Rhubarb Sorbet

Veal Medallions with Cabernet & Green Peppercorns
Paul Thomas Washington Cabernet Sauvignon

OR

Beef on a String
Quilceda Creek Washington Cabernet Sauvignon

Chocolate Marquise

OR

Cappuccino Ice Cream Tart

Paul Thomas
Salmon Bay
Quilceda Creek

Washington State has long been the nation's third largest grape growing region, just behind California and New York. Until the sixties, however, most of the varieties grown here were mainly Concords, Vitis labrusca, *and were used for grape juice or fortified wines.*

Today's burgeoning wine industry owes its birth to a group of wine-loving academics in Seattle. In the late fifties, Lloyd Woodburne, from the University of Washington, purchased wine varietal grapes, Vinas vinifera, *from Columbia Valley growers and with some of his university colleagues began making wine in his garage. They bought a small vineyard in the Yakima Valley, and became a bonded winery under the name of Associated Vintners. In 1967, at the urging of Leon Adams, an authority on American wines, they leased a warehouse east of Seattle and offered their wines commercially. Their wines from Associated Vintners quickly became popular and won several major awards.*

By 1980, Associated Vintners was in the awkward position of being too small to survive in an increasingly competitive market and too big to be run by committee. They brought in new investors, increased their capacity, and most importantly, perhaps, hired David Lake, winemaker. In 1984 they changed the name to Columbia Winery.

Lake, a Canadian, had spent ten years in the British wine trade and had qualified as a Master of Wine. Completing studies at the University of California at Davis, the most prestigious enology and viticulture school in the country, he became assistant to David Lett at Eyrie Vineyards in Oregon. When David Lett recommended David Lake to Associated Vintners, Lake was one of only ten Masters of Wine working in this country, and the only one in the Northwest. His palate enabled him to distinguish the highest quality grapes and identify the best blends to produce consistently fine wines. His arrival added respectability and seriousness to the state's young industry.

The first time I met David, Robert Rossellini, my boss at the legendary Other Place Restaurant in Seattle, had announced that the new winemaker at Associated Vintners would attend one of our weekly professional wine tastings. Impressed by his credentials, the rest of us were careful to discover what David thought before we revealed our own impressions. He attended our wine tastings regularly and we took the sessions very seriously when he was there.

After Ann and I moved to Seaview, we maintained contact with David. Delightful, affable, and modest, he came often with his wife Connie to the Inn and restaurant, so when we began our series of Northwest winemakers' dinners, David was one of the first people we invited.

Smoked Salmon-Whitefish Sausage

6 oz smoked salmon
¼ lb salmon fillet
½ lb Petrale sole
1½ tsp garlic, minced (**3** cloves)
½ tsp salt
1 dash Tabasco
1½ tsp fresh lemon juice
¼ tsp white pepper
2 egg whites
¾ c heavy cream
2 oz clarified butter
½ c Basil Mayonnaise

Salmon Bay Winery
Oyster Shell White
When I was in charge of the wine program at the now-legendary Rosellini's Other Place in Seattle, Bruce Crabtree was my counterpart at our sister restaurant, the Four 10. He turned an amateur winemaking hobby into a full-fledged business, and now produces some very appealing wines. One of his most popular examples is this Semillon, which accompanies seafood (and especially shellfish, as the name implies) beautifully.

Make sure all of the fish has all the bones completely removed. Finely chop 2 ounces of the smoked salmon and set it aside.

Cut the sole and salmon into 1-inch pieces and place them with the remaining smoked salmon, garlic, salt, Tabasco, lemon juice and pepper in a food processor and blend until smooth. Add the egg whites and pulse just until incorporated. *Do not overmix.* Remove the mixture to a mixing bowl. Stir in the reserved minced smoked salmon.

Add the cream ¼ cup at a time, folding gently until it is completely incorporated. Chill several hours or overnight. Press plastic wrap onto the mixture to prevent a skin from forming.

On a long counter, lay out a long piece of cheesecloth and butter the bottom third of its entire length. Pipe or spoon the fish mixture along the bottom edge of the cheesecloth, leaving about 1 inch at the bottom. Make the sausages to any length–*4 inch lengths work best*–but leave about 2 inches between

continued...

SMOKED SALMON-WHITEFISH SAUSAGE

...continued

each one. Roll up the cheesecloth and tie the ends between the sausages. Cut into separate sausages.

Poach the sausages in a *court bouillon* (or water) until they are just firm, about 5 minutes.

Serve this sausage hot or cold with the fresh BASIL MAYONNAISE.

Makes 14 small sausages.

Sometimes it's hard to know whether you're reading a house address or date of construction as you stroll through sleepy Seaview on a summer's evening, listening to the ocean, smelling the air, recalling the meal you just finished.

BASIL MAYONNAISE

¼ c fresh basil, finely chopped
1 Tb white wine vinegar
1 c mayonnaise

In a food processor, process the basil and vinegar until completely blended.

Add the mayonnaise and blend until incorporated.

Makes 1 cup.

SMOKED SALMON MOUSSE

2 oz smoked salmon
3 oz cooked salmon
1 lb cream cheese, softened
2 Tb heavy cream
2 Tb Scotch whisky
4 tsp tarragon vinegar
4 tsp fresh tarragon, chopped

Dice 1 ounce of the smoked salmon and set aside. Combine the remaining smoked salmon with the rest of the ingredients in a food processor and process until it is a smooth paste.

Remove to a clean bowl and fold in the diced salmon by hand. Cover and chill for several hours.

Serve with crackers, cucumber slices or crisp snow peas.

Makes 3 cups.

Paul Thomas Washington Chardonnay

Paul Thomas made his name in Washington State by producing the first good examples of dry fruit wines. He slowly but very successfully ventured into wine varietals, eventually making everything but Chardonnay. Just a few years ago, he finally started releasing Chardonnays, which quickly became known as some of the most delicious in the state, a fine match for some of the state's favorite salmon.

This can be an impressive buffet dish when shaped into a fish and decorated with thinly sliced cucumber "scales," caper "eyes" and cucumber "fins" or you can use lemon slices, pimientos or black olives.

SHOALWATER FRENCH BREAD

2 ½ c water, 95°

⅛ c dry yeast

1 Tb sugar

1 Tb salt

1 Tb salad oil

4 egg whites

7-8 c all purpose flour

1 egg yolk

In a large mixing bowl, place in this order the water, yeast, sugar, salt and oil. Allow to stand for 5 minutes.

Add the egg whites and flour. With the mixer on low, use the dough hook and mix, watching closely. Add additional flour, if necessary, to make a soft but not sticky dough.

Knead for 10 minutes.

Place the dough in an oiled bowl, turning it to coat all surfaces. Cover it with a clean towel and allow it to rise in a warm place until doubled in bulk, about 1 hour.

Turn out onto counter and divide in half. Roll into balls, cover and allow them to rise for 30 minutes.

Roll each ball into a thick rectangle, about 8 by 10 inches. Roll them jellyroll style from the long side, pressing the dough into itself on each turn. Pinch the ends of the loaf and place them in an oiled French bread pan. Allow the loaves to rise for another 20 minutes.

Cut 3 diagonal slits in the top of each loaf with a sharp knife, then brush with a mixture of 1 egg yolk and 2 tablespoons of water. Bake in a preheated 400° oven until golden brown on the bottom as well as on the top, about 20 to 30 minutes.

Makes 2 loaves.

Orange-Saffron-Tomato Cod

3 shallots, minced

3 roma tomatoes, sliced

3 Tb orange juice concentrate

3 Tb red wine vinegar

⅓ c white wine

½ tsp saffron

¼ tsp sugar (or to taste)

1¼ c butter,
chilled & cut in ½-inch cubes

6 7-oz True Cod or Yelloweye Rockfish fillets

1 orange, for garnish

Salmon Bay Winery
Washington Chardonnay
Salmon Bay also produces an excellent Chardonnay and Cabernet Sauvignon. Bruce's medium-bodied and pretty Chardonnay is a lovely accompaniment for our many delicate Pacific whitefish, such as True Cod. This wine with this dish is an excellent example of a great marriage.

Put the shallots, tomatoes, orange juice concentrate, vinegar, wine, saffron and sugar in a sauce pan. Simmer, covered, until the tomatoes fall apart, then remove the lid and reduce it to ⅓ cup.

Purée the sauce and put it through a fine-mesh strainer.

Put the purée in a clean sauce pan and bring it to a boil, stirring constantly. When it boils, remove from heat and add butter bit by bit, stirring constantly. Hold the finished sauce in a warm water bath.

Bake the cod in a preheated 500° oven until it is firm to the touch, about 6 to 8 minutes.

Ladle the sauce onto warm plates and place the fish on top. Garnish with orange slices or zest.

Makes 6 servings.

Cheri's favorite cod is True, or Pacific, Cod. It has a very large flake and a beautiful white meat – striking served against a colorful sauce.

Wild Mushroom-Sake Sturgeon

Paul Thomas Reserve Chardonnay

Paul Thomas has recently sold his interest in the winery, but the wines continue to be made by his very capable winemaker, Mark Cave. Mark took over winemaking duties from Brian Carter, who made the first exceptional Paul Thomas Reserve Chardonnay. This very Burgundian, barrel-fermented wine continues to impress year after year, and only gets better with age. Sturgeon, wild mushrooms and sake combine in an explosion of flavors which demands a wine as full as this.

2 Tb sesame oil

1 Tb garlic, minced

3 oz boletus mushrooms, sliced

3 oz *lacterious deliciosas* mushrooms, sliced

3 oz cauliflower mushrooms, sliced

3 oz matsutake mushrooms, sliced

¼ c soy sauce

2 c sake

2 c fish stock

2 c white wine

1 c butter, chilled & cut into bits

6 7-oz sturgeon fillets

Heat the sesame oil over medium heat in a medium sauce pan, add the garlic and sauté until golden. Add the sliced mushrooms and sauté until tender.

Deglaze the mushrooms with the soy sauce and toss to combine. Add sake, fish stock and 1 cup of the wine and bring to a low boil. Simmer for 15 minutes. Remove the mushrooms with a slotted spoon to a warm dish and reserve. Reduce the liquids to 1 cup.

Remove the reduced liquid from the heat and immediately begin incorporating the butter into the reduction, bit by bit, whisking continuously. Hold the sauce at a constant temperature until ready to use, preferably in a double boiler over warm—*not hot*—water.

Place the sturgeon fillets in a baking dish in a single layer. Add the remaining 1 cup of wine and bake in a preheated 500° oven until the fish is firm and resilient to the touch, about 10 to 12 minutes.

To serve, ladle ¼ cup of sauce on each plate, top with the fillets and garnish with the reserved warm mushrooms.

Makes 6 servings.

RHUBARB SORBET

3⅓ c sugar
2⅔ c water
8 c fresh rhubarb, sliced
½ c water

Bring sugar and 2⅔ cups of water to a full boil. Remove from heat immediately. Refrigerate until chilled.

Place the rhubarb and ½ cup of water in a baking dish. Cover with foil and poach for 45 minutes in a preheated 350° oven. The rhubarb should be soft, but still hold its shape. Chill.

Add chilled sugar syrup to the rhubarb and process in an ice cream freezer according to manufacturer's instructions. *The rhubarb will break up in the freezing process.* Serve the sorbet the same day it is made.

Makes 8 servings.

This sorbet is a show-stopping pink and has a glorious creamy texture. Top it with fresh spring strawberries for a light low-fat dessert or include it as a palate cleanser.

VEAL MEDALLIONS
WITH
CABERNET & GREEN PEPPERCORNS

Paul Thomas Washington Cabernet Sauvignon
Another varietal in which Paul Thomas wines excel, producing well-balanced, richly flavored, dense Cabernets. Serve with Veal Medallions, a lovely food-wine combination which shows how well one enhances the other.

½ lb bacon

2 c Cabernet Sauvignon

2 c veal demi-glace (**4 c** SHOALWATER VEAL STOCK reduced to 2 c)

1 oz green peppercorns

1 shallot, minced

3 Tb pinenuts

2 c heavy cream

4 Tb (2 oz) bleu cheese, crumbled

salt & pepper, to taste

3 lb veal tenderloin, trimmed & sliced into ½-inch thick medallions

Slice the bacon into narrow diagonal strips and fry in a sauté pan until they are crisp. Drain and crumble the bacon in bits when it has cooled. Reserve both the bacon and the drippings.

Combine the wine, demi-glace, green peppercorns, shallot, pinenuts and half of the reserved bacon in a sauce pan. Bring it to a boil and reduce until it turns syrupy, to about 1 cup. *Watch it closely to keep it from burning.*

Add the cream to the sauce and reduce it to about 2 cups. Add the bleu cheese and stir until melted. Season with salt and pepper and hold the sauce over warm water while preparing the veal.

Place 2 tablespoons of the bacon drippings in a sauté pan over high heat and sauté the medallions until browned on both sides and medium-rare inside.

Ladle the sauce on each plate and place medallions on top. Garnish with the remaining reserved bacon bits.

Makes 6 servings.

Beef on a String

1 sprig rosemary (or **½ tsp** dried)
2 sprigs thyme (or **1 tsp** dried)
4 sprigs parsley
2 bay leaves
2 tsp marjoram
1 Tb black peppercorns
1½-2 lb tenderloin of beef,
trimmed & cut into 4 roasts
8 c Shoalwater Veal Stock
20 pearl onions, peeled
5 turnips, cut into 20 pieces about
¼ inch by ¼ inch by 2 inches
12 baby carrots
(or 12 pieces sliced on the diagonal)
8 red potatoes, as small as possible
4 **3-inch stalks** celery
4 cloves garlic, peeled & bruised

Quilceda Creek Washington Cabernet Sauvignon
Alex Golitzin is one of the legendary figures in the Washington wine industry and heads up the only one-wine winery in the state. But the one wine he makes, Cabernet Sauvignon, is one of the best and most sought-after in the region. He packs a lot of flavor and complexity into each bottling, and makes it to last (and improve) many years. A rich wine for a rich entrée.

Make a *bouquet garni* (a bundle) of the herbs and peppercorns in a cheesecloth.

Tie the individual roasts with butcher's twine, making a "handle" in the center with the two ends of the twine.

In a large pot, bring the stock to a boil. Reduce the heat, add the *bouquet garni* and pearl onions and simmer for 10 minutes.

Add the remaining vegetables. Use a long spoon handle, dowel or ruler to suspend the roasts in the liquid so they are covered, but do not touch the bottom. Simmer for 12 to 15 minutes.

Remove the twine and let the meat rest on a warmed platter. Distribute the vegetables among warmed plates.

continued...

BEEF ON A STRING

...continued

In a sauce pan, reduce 4 cups of the poaching liquid to 1 cup.

Slice the beef, arrange the slices on the plates with the vegetables and pour the reduced stock over them.

Makes 4 servings.

Chocolate Marquise

4 pt strawberries
¼ c water
sugar, to taste
14 oz bittersweet chocolate
¾ c sugar (super-fine will dissolve more quickly)
1 c unsalted butter
½ c unsweetened cocoa
8 eggs, separated
2 Tb strawberry liqueur (or brandy)

Rinse the berries and reserve the 12 nicest ones for garnish. Process the remaining berries in a blender with the water and some sugar, depending on the sweetness of the berries, until smooth.

Pass through a strainer to remove the seeds. Set aside.

In a double boiler or microwave, melt together the chocolate, ¾ cup of sugar and butter until smooth. *Be sure not to heat too fast.* Stir frequently—this will take a while so you'll have to be patient.

When melted, stir in the cocoa.

Separate the eggs into two mixing bowls.

Lightly mix the egg yolks and slowly add the warm chocolate mixture, beating constantly.

When well mixed, transfer the mixture to a medium sauce pan and cook over low heat, whisking continually until sugar dissolves, about 6 minutes.

Beat the egg whites until soft peaks form.

Fold together the chocolate mixture and the egg whites.

Fold in the liqueur.

continued...

Chocolate Marquise

...continued

Pour into an oiled and lined 9 by 5 inch loaf pan. Tap the pan sharply to eliminate large air bubbles and then cover with plastic wrap. Place in the freezer for at least 4 hours or overnight.

To remove the marquise from the pan, place the pan *briefly* in hot water. Turn out onto serving platter.

To serve, place a pool of strawberry purée on each plate. Slice the marquise into ½ inch slices and set in purée. Garnish with a fresh berry.

Makes 12 to 14 servings.

CHARDONNAY

Cappuccino Ice Cream Tart

1 c almonds, toasted & coarsely chopped

3/4 c flour

1 c sugar

1 tsp cinnamon

4 Tb butter

1 egg

4 oz semisweet chocolate, coarsely chopped

3 c heavy cream

6 egg yolks

2 Tb coffee crystals

4 tsp unsweetened cocoa powder

shaved chocolate, for garnish

Put the almonds, flour, 1/4 cup of the sugar and 1/2 teaspoon of the cinnamon in a food processor and process until finely ground. Add the butter and pulse until it is well incorporated. Add the egg and blend until the mixture clumps together. Remove the dough.

Lightly butter a 10-inch tart pan with a removable bottom and press the nut dough into the pan and around the edges. Freeze until firm.

Press aluminum foil into the tart shell and fill with pie weights. Bake in a preheated 400° oven for 20 minutes, remove the weights and foil and bake until done, about another 5 to 10 minutes.

Sprinkle the chocolate over the bottom of the crust while the crust is still hot and spread it with a pastry brush as it melts. Set the crust aside.

Beat the cream with 1/2 cup of the sugar until it forms soft mounds.

continued...

CAPPUCCINO ICE CREAM TART

...continued

In a separate bowl, beat the egg yolks and the remaining $\frac{1}{4}$ cup of sugar until they are pale and thick. Add the coffee, cocoa and the remaining $\frac{1}{2}$ teaspoon of cinnamon. Mix well.

Fold the egg mixture into the cream. Blend until incorporated and refrigerate until well chilled.

Freeze this mixture in an ice cream machine, stopping while it is still a bit soft. Smooth into the crust, mounding it slightly in the center. Freeze overnight.

Serve directly from the freezer, garnished with shaved chocolate.

Makes 1 tart.

CAMERON
PANTHER CREEK
SALISHAN
ARTERBERRY

DUCK LIVER PÂTÉ
Panther Creek Cellars Willamette Valley Melon

CUCUMBER-DILL HALIBUT
Salishan Vineyards Washington Dry White Riesling

PEAR SAGE CHICKEN
Cameron Winery Willamette Valley Pinot Noir

OR

PECAN CHICKEN
Panther Creek Cellars Willamette Valley Pinot Noir

PESTO STUFFED FLANK STEAK
Arterberry Winery Willamette Valley Pinot Noir

RASPBERRY MERINGUE NESTS

Cameron
Panther Creek
Salishan
Arterberry

What distinguished the young regional wine scene of the 1970s was the friendliness, earnestness and genuineness of its major players. I found all the regional winemakers to be delightful, down-home and individualistic people, truly interested in producing high-quality wines to please a discriminating audience. An enthusiastic lot, they actually listened to opinions and criticism, admitted mistakes and laughed about some of their "interesting" early experiments. They clearly enjoyed the creative ground-breaking process.

The handful of Pacific Northwest wineries which got started in the late 1960s and early 1970s has now grown to almost 200 enterprises in Washington, Oregon and Idaho. Some of them have grown significantly over the past twenty years, but even the largest winery in the region, Columbia Crest, is no bigger than any number of medium-sized California producers—and most remain as small operations, where the owner and/or winemaker is often in the tasting rooms.

The proliferation of wineries as well as twenty years of winemaking experience in the region has resulted in a sophisticated industry of delicious, complex and technically correct wines. As a whole, Pacific Northwest wines have never been better—and they continue to improve. Although much experimentation still goes on, such as Columbia's stellar first release of a powerful Rhône-style Syrah in 1991, the industry has learned a lot in a relatively short time about which grapes grow best in which places and under what conditions. Cabernet Sauvignon has obviously found its niche in Washington State, with countless excellent bottlings such as the single-vineyard Cabernets from Columbia and Chateau Ste. Michelle. Superb Merlots from the state, like those produced at Chinook Wines or Leonetti Cellar, now deserve equal billing with Cabernet. Pinot Noir has certainly become the jewel of Oregon, with delicious examples offered by every self-respecting winery in the state where some of the best are made at Eyrie and Amity Vineyards. Rieslings, which grow very well in the entire region and once were more or less divided between the fuller, sweeter ones of Washington and the leaner, drier ones of Oregon, now all appear to be going very dry (with a few lovely late-harvest exceptions) to take on the national Chardonnay explosion. Speaking of Chardonnay, in good years the region produces some superb ones, such as Woodward Canyon's Winemaker's Reserve and Tualatin's Private Reserve. Pinot Gris, once an unknown Alsatian blending grape planted in the region in minute quantity by David Lett at Eyrie Vineyards, has suddenly become the hottest dry white wine commodity in Oregon.

DUCK LIVER PÂTÉ

10 oz duck livers
10 oz chicken livers
½ c heavy cream
1 Tb black pepper
1 c brandy
20 oz fatback
10 oz pork, ground
½ c Port
½ c crème fraîche
4 eggs
½ tsp juniper berries, crushed
1 Tb EPICES FINES
1 tsp kosher salt
1 tsp white pepper
1 c blueberries
1 c cranberries

Panther Creek Cellars
Willamette Valley Melon
Ken Wright is one of the bright young stars on the Oregon wine scene, producing some of the most interesting Pinot Noirs in the state for the past few years. He recently introduced a limited release of a little known Loire Valley varietal called Melon (made in this country previously, and inaccurately, as Pinot Blanc), which produces a delightful, dry but opulent, Chardonnay-like wine. Match it with The Shoalwater's Duck Liver Pâté for a fine light meal or appetizer.

Marinate the duck and chicken livers in cream, pepper and ½ cup of the brandy overnight.

Thinly slice 10 ounces of the fatback. Use it to line a 13 by 4 by 4 inch mold, making sure you have enough left to cover the top. Refrigerate.

Finely dice the remaining 10 ounces of fatback and blend it with the ground pork in a food processor until smooth and creamy. Blend in the remaining ½ cup of brandy, Port, crème fraîche and eggs. Add spices, salt and pepper. Blend, but do not overprocess. Rinse livers and add to forcemeat, blending well.

Alternate layers of forcemeat and berries in the mold. Finish with a layer of fatback. Cover with foil and weight the top with pie weights. Place in a hot water bath that comes two thirds of the way up the sides of the mold.

continued...

DUCK LIVER PÂTÉ

...continued

When making the forcemeat for this or any pâté, overseason the mixture; the flavors will leach out a bit when the meat cooks.

Leave the pie weights on and refrigerate overnight. Remove weights and mold only when completely chilled.

Slice into 20 pieces. Serve with cranberry chutney, pickled asparagus and fresh French bread.

Makes 20 slices.

EPICES FINES

1 Tb bay leaf, ground
1 Tb thyme, ground
1 Tb cloves, ground
1 Tb nutmeg, ground
1 Tb cinnamon, ground
1 Tb mace, ground
1 Tb paprika, ground
1½ tsp marjoram, ground
1½ tsp oregano, ground
1½ tsp basil, ground
1½ tsp ginger, ground
1½ tsp sage, ground
1½ tsp allspice, ground
1 tsp white pepper, ground
1 tsp black pepper, ground

This herb and spice blend is wonderful in pâtés, sausages, marinades and salad dressings…let your imagination supply the rest. For a very fresh flavor, buy whole ingredients and grind them in a coffee grinder, spice mill or blender.

Makes ½ cup.

DUCK LIVER PÂTÉ

CRANBERRY CHUTNEY

4 c cranberries
1 c raisins
1½ c sugar
2 tsp cinnamon
1½ tsp ginger
¼ tsp cloves
1 c water
½ c onion, finely chopped
½ c green apple, finely chopped
½ c celery, finely chopped

Put the cranberries, raisins, sugar, spices, and water in a medium sauce pan. Bring to a boil, reduce heat, and simmer until berries pop, about 15 minutes.

Add the onion, apple and celery. Simmer until the mixture thickens, about 15 minutes.

Cool and refrigerate.

Makes 4 cups.

CUCUMBER-DILL HALIBUT

6 6-oz halibut fillets
1 c DILL PESTO
1 c white wine
1½ c CUCUMBER MAYONNAISE
¾ c MELON RELISH, for garnish

Salishan Vineyards Washington Dry White Riesling
Salishan Vineyards, in La Center, Washington, is the closest vinifera winery to our restaurant (about 1-½ hours away near I-5) so we think of it as our neighborhood winery. Joan Wolverton, owner-winemaker, is also the kind of person anyone would want for a neighbor—a delightful, unassuming, straightforward individual who also makes delightful wines (and even tells you when she thinks one didn't turn out). Her Dry Riesling is one of her specialties and makes Cheri's Cucumber Dill Halibut taste even better.

Make three diagonal slits in the top of each fillet and fill with Dill Pesto.

Pour the wine into a shallow baking pan, lay in the fillets and bake in a preheated 500° oven until done, about 10 to 12 minutes.

Pool ¼ cup of the CUCUMBER MAYONNAISE on each plate, top with the halibut and garnish with the MELON RELISH. *The Melon Relish looks great when held in a small steamed zucchini "boat" or a 1-inch hollowed out slice.*

Makes 6 servings.

DILL PESTO

This is a wonderful variation on the more usual basil pesto. It is particularly nice with grilled fish.

½ c dill weed, finely chopped
4 c spinach, stems removed, packed medium-firm
1 Tb garlic, minced
1 Tb Dijon mustard
1 tsp pepper
1 c Parmesan cheese
¼ c olive oil

continued...

CUCUMBER-DILL HALIBUT

...continued

This pesto will keep for up to a month refrigerated in a covered container. It may also be made without the cheese and frozen, airtight, for up to a year. Defrost in the refrigerator and stir in the cheese before using.

Blend the dill, spinach, garlic, mustard and pepper in a food processor. Add the Parmesan and blend to a smooth paste. Add the olive oil slowly with processor still running.

Makes 2½ cups.

CUCUMBER MAYONNAISE

This is a refreshing dip for vegetables or melon slices, and a nice alternative to tartar sauce for oysters or fish & chips.

1 large cucumber, halved & seeded
½ small red onion
1 sprig parsley
1½ tsp rice wine vinegar
1 Tb Riesling wine
1 Tb SHOALWATER SHRIMP STOCK
1 c mayonnaise

Since the skin adds color and flavor to the mayonnaise, don't peel the cucumbers.

Combine all the ingredients except the mayonnaise in a food processor or blender and purée until smooth and creamy.

Blend in the mayonnaise and refrigerate.

Makes 2 ½ cups.

CUCUMBER-DILL HALIBUT

MELON RELISH

2 roma tomatoes
¼ cantaloupe
⅛ honeydew melon
1 large cucumber
1 tsp balsamic vinegar
1 Tb fresh dill weed, chopped
¼ tsp salt
⅛ tsp pepper

Cut the tomatoes, melons and cucumbers into uniform dice, about the size of corn kernels.

Toss with the vinegar, dill, salt and pepper. Cover and refrigerate. Marinate at least 8 hours or overnight before using.

Makes 3 cups.

This is a nice accompaniment with sauteed chanterelle mushrooms; or serve it with ham or prosciutto.

PEAR SAGE CHICKEN

2 pears, peeled, cored & diced
¼ c water
1½ c chicken stock
4 Tb brandy
4 Tb pear liqueur
1 Tb balsamic vinegar
1 tsp dried sage
½ tsp salt
4 chicken breasts, bone-in
flour, to coat chicken
11 Tb butter
3 Tb salad oil
1 c BACON VINAIGRETTE
1 bunch kale, trimmed & cleaned
½ red onion, thinly sliced
¼ lb bacon, fried, drained & crumbled into bits

Cameron Winery Willamette Valley Pinot Noir
John Paul quickly established a fine reputation among more veteran Oregon winemakers for producing high-quality, clean-flavored Chardonnay and Pinot Noir in the Burgundy tradition. A soft-spoken, earnest young man, his Pinot Noirs are generally intensely-styled wines whose flavors get bigger and better with bottle aging. We like his Pinots especially with the muskiness of the chicken preparation.

Put the pears and water in a covered sauce pan over low heat and cook until the pears fall apart. Purée and strain.

In another small sauce pan reduce chicken stock over high heat to just over ¾ cup.

Combine the stock and pear purée in a sauce pan. Add the brandy, liqueur, vinegar and sage. Bring the pear glaze to a boil and reduce it to 1½ cups. Slowly stir in 8 tablespoons of the butter and remove from the heat. Add the salt and hold over warm water while finishing the dish.

Dust the chicken lightly in flour. Melt the remaining 3 tablespoons of butter with the salad oil in a sauté pan and brown the chicken breasts over high heat. Transfer to a roasting pan and roast in a preheated

We use this recipe with poussin at the restaurant. It would also be excellent with Cornish Game hens, or you could simply split a chicken in half and grill it.

continued...

PEAR SAGE CHICKEN

...continued

500° oven until the juices run clear, about 12 to 15 minutes.

Warm the BACON VINAIGRETTE. Toss the kale, onion and bacon in the vinaigrette until the kale is slightly wilted. Arrange beds of kale on serving plates and top with the chicken. Pour the hot glaze over and serve immediately.

Makes 4 servings.

PEAR SAGE CHICKEN

BACON VINAIGRETTE

¼ lb bacon
½ c salad oil
½ c raspberry wine vinegar
½ tsp thyme
½ tsp kosher salt
¼ tsp allspice

Sauté the bacon and reserve ½ cup of the drippings. When cool, crumble the bacon into bits and set aside for tossing with salad greens.

Over medium heat, whisk together the ½ cup of bacon drippings, salad oil, vinegar, thyme, salt and allspice until blended.

Use the dressing warm or cool to room temperature, cover and refrigerate. To use, heat through and toss with selected greens and reserved bacon pieces.

This is a wonderful dressing for a warm spinach salad. Add to the spinach some chopped, hard-boiled egg, bacon bits, thinly sliced sweet onion and Parmesan cheese and toss quickly with the warm dressing.

Makes 1 cup.

PECAN CHICKEN

Panther Creek Cellars
Willamette Valley Pinot Noir
I don't usually buy a wine for its label, but this is one in which the winery name (and its great black label) actually suggests the liquid in the bottle. When I think of Ken Wright's Pinot Noirs, I think sleek, smooth, powerful, graceful, in a word, feline. Ann loves it with our classic Pecan Chicken.

¾ c butter, softened
½ c Dijon mustard
6 boneless chicken breasts
1 lb pecans, finely chopped
6 Tb clarified butter
1 c sour cream
1 c heavy cream

Cream together butter and ¼ cup of the mustard. The mixture should be very soft—almost liquid—and well blended.

Flatten the chicken breasts with a mallet. Pat them very dry. Coat one side of the chicken well with the butter-mustard mixture and press that side into the pecans. Repeat for other side.

Heat the clarified butter in a large skillet. Brown both sides of the chicken over medium-high heat, turning only once. Transfer the chicken to a baking dish, reserving pan juices and any nuts in the skillet.

Bake the chicken in a preheated 450° oven until done, about 8 to 10 minutes.

Drain excess oil from skillet. Over medium heat, whisk together the sour cream, the remaining ¼ cup of mustard and heavy cream. Heat gently—*do not boil.*

Serve the chicken on heated plates with the sauce spooned over the top.

Makes 6 servings.

PESTO STUFFED FLANK STEAK

Arterberry Winery Willamette Valley Pinot Noir
The Oregon wine industry lost one of its finest (and nicest) young winemakers when Fred Arterberry died last year. But his reputation and the wines he made, particularly the Pinot Noirs from the past few years, live on and keep improving as excellent examples of those wines. We enjoyed knowing him over the years as one of the friendliest people in the business, who really exemplified the one on one quality which characterizes so much of the wine trade in the Northwest.

1 oz fresh basil, chopped
½ c olive oil
1 clove garlic, minced
½ c tomato juice
½ c red wine
1 bay leaf
2 tsp black pepper
2 lb flank steak
2 c bread crumbs
½ lb cream cheese
1 c PESTO
⅓ c Parmesan cheese, grated
oil, for browning steaks
2 c TOMATO, MERLOT & ROASTED GARLIC CREAM SAUCE

Combine the basil, olive oil, garlic, tomato juice, red wine, bay leaf and black pepper. Pour over the flank steak and marinate in the refrigerator overnight.

Blend together the bread crumbs, cream cheese, Pesto and Parmesan.

Remove the flank steak from the marinade and pat it dry. *Make sure you have a really sharp knife on hand, it will make this next step much easier.* With the steak flat on a cutting board, carefully cut into it from the side, parallel with the grain. Fold the top back as you cut until the steak is laid out flat like an open book—*don't cut all the way through.* Press the stuffing firmly onto the meat and roll it up like a jellyroll, so the grain runs lengthwise. Tie it at several spots with butcher's twine.

Heat enough oil in a heavy pan to brown the meat on all sides.

continued...

STUFFED FLANK STEAK

...continued

Put it in a roasting pan and cook it in a preheated 500° oven until a meat thermometer registers 120°, about 20 to 25 minutes.

Let it set for about 5 minutes after removing it from the oven. Slice and serve with warmed TOMATO, MERLOT & ROASTED GARLIC CREAM SAUCE.

Makes 6 servings.

PESTO

4 bunches basil (about **2 c** leaves), as fresh as possible
1 Tb garlic, minced
¼ c pinenuts
1½ tsp salt
½ c olive oil
2 Tb butter, softened
¾ c Parmesan cheese

Combine basil, garlic, pinenuts and salt in a blender or food processor.

With machine running, slowly pour in the olive oil. Stop the machine and scrape down the sides occasionally.

Remove to a bowl and stir in the butter and Parmesan by hand.

Makes 2 cups.

When basil comes into season I rush to my stove to make gnocchi or fresh pasta topped with the fresh pesto. However, don't fail to try pesto added to soups, steamed clams or fish, mayonnaise or hollandaise sauce. To freeze pesto for use later in the season, leave out the butter and cheese. Defrost the pesto in the refrigerator, beat in the butter and cheese and serve. If the pesto seems too thick, thin it with a bit of hot water.

Stuffed Flank Steak

Tomato, Merlot & Roasted Garlic Cream Sauce

1 shallot, minced
2 Tb butter
2 Tb Roasted Garlic
1 tsp salt
½ tsp pepper
1 tsp basil
2 Tb brandy
2 c Merlot
2 c veal demi-glace (**4 c** Shoalwater Veal Stock reduced to 2 c)
½ c heavy cream
⅓ c tomato paste

Sauté the shallot in 1 tablespoon of the butter until it begins to brown. Add the garlic, mashing the mixture with the back of a spoon. Add salt, pepper and basil and deglaze the pan with the brandy.

Add the Merlot and reduce the sauce to about 1 cup. Add the demi-glace and continue to reduce to about 2 cups. Add the cream and reduce again to 2 cups.

Stir in the tomato paste. When the sauce reaches a boil, remove it from the heat and stir in the remaining 1 tablespoon of butter.

Makes 2 cups.

RASPBERRY MERINGUE NESTS

4 egg whites

pinch salt

1 c sugar

2 pt raspberries

4 oz semisweet chocolate

½ c heavy cream

whipped cream, for garnish

In a clean bowl, whip the egg whites with the salt until they begin to stiffen. Slowly whip in the sugar, a tablespoon at a time, and beat until the whites are stiff and glossy.

Place a sheet of parchment paper on a cookie sheet. Place a second cookie sheet under the first to prevent the meringues from browning on the bottom. Draw six 4-inch circles on the parchment.

Fill a large pastry bag fitted with a star tip with the meringue. Pipe the meringue into the circles, beginning at the center and spiraling outward. As you reach each edge, begin building a wall by spiralling upward two layers, making nests.

Bake in a preheated 250° oven until firm and dry all the way through, 45 to 75 minutes, depending on the humidity. Remove and cool.

Purée 1 pint of the raspberries with sugar to taste. Strain out the seeds and set aside.

Melt the chocolate with the cream. Beat with a whisk until blended. Cool until it reaches room temperature and begins to thicken. Pour about 2 tablespoons into each shell to cover the bottom.

Ladle the raspberry purée onto serving plates and place the nests on top. Use the remaining pint of raspberries to fill each nest. Top with a rosette of whipped cream.

Makes 6 servings. 

Staton Hills
Blackwood Canyon
Bonair
Portteus

Grilled Duck Sausage
Blackwood Canyon Winery Washington Semillon

OR

Escargots
Bonair Winery Chateau Puryear Vineyard Chardonnay

Cranberry Champagne Soup
Staton Hills Vineyards Washington Johannisberg Riesling

OR

Six-Onion Soup
Portteus Vineyards Yakima Valley Chardonnay

Chanterelle-Port Sturgeon
Staton Hills Vineyards Washington Pinot Noir

Hazelnut & Cabernet Veal
Portteus Vineyards Yakima Valley Cabernet Sauvignon

Cranberry-Swirl Cheesecake
Blackwood Canyon Ultra Late Harvest Reisling

STATON HILLS
BLACKWOOD CANYON
BONAIR
PORTTEUS

In our opinion, wine is primarily a beverage meant to be enjoyed in the company of good food. Our aim with these dinners is to create a win-win situation for the winery and for the restaurant. The trick is always to produce the proper balance: We neither want to overwhelm a wine with too many discordant or overly-intense flavors in the food, nor do we want the wine to be so powerful as to leave one wondering how the food tasted.

I can laugh now remembering one time I neglected to do my homework and got caught. When Dick and Nancy Ponzi came to do a dinner, I trusted my previous experience and asssumed I knew the style of their Pinot Noirs. I remembered their red wines to be elegant and complex, but on the light side in body, reminiscent of the Burgundian wines from the Côte de Beaune. I conveyed this impression to the staff at our many discussions, and we agreed on a preparation of pork to accompany the Pinot Noir 1985 which they were bringing—and which I had not tasted. When Dick Ponzi stood up to make a few introductory remarks at the dinner, he spoke of the Pinot Noir 1985 without first looking at the menu. He began confidently, "This wine is no lightweight and will not do well with most preparations of chicken or light meats, such as pork. It calls for a much stronger-flavored meat, like lamb or venison!" He was right, of course, and got to prove it.

There is an undefinable, almost magical quality to these special dinners that allows even such mistakes to work. The dinners usually involve 25 to 40 people whom we seat randomly in groups of six to ten. In very short order, animated conversations between relative strangers begin to occur (This may or may not have anything to do with food or wine.) and new friendships emerge. These people are drawn together by one common bond: the love of fine food and wine, which promotes good fellowship.

We usually suggest to the winemaker that any remarks to the entire group be made at the beginning of the meal, as it is usually very difficult to get a word in edgewise later on. The camaraderie that develops at each dinner is delightful to observe and makes all the work that goes into the dinners worthwhile.

Grilled Duck Sausage

5 lb duck meat, skinned and deboned, cut across the grain into ½-inch cubes
5 lb ground pork
4 lb fat back, minced
5 c blueberries
5 c cranberries
1⅓ c Port
¼ c Triple Sec liqueur (or Grand Marnier)
¼ c garlic, finely chopped
¾ c honey
1 Tb juniper berries, ground
1 Tb ground ginger
¼ c Epices Fines herb blend
4 Tb + 2 tsp kosher salt
pork casings, if making links

When you cut the duck meat, be sure to check for bone or gristle.

To mince the back fat as fine as possible, freeze it first. Mince by hand; a food processor will tend to blend it into a paste.

Mix all the ingredients (except the casings) together and let them marinate overnight.

Run the mixture through a meat grinder, using a medium blade.

Use the sausage as is to make patties, or make links using the sausage stuffing attachment on your mixer, using the largest holes on this attachment.

This sausage freezes beautifully.

Makes 15 pounds.

Blackwood Canyon Winery Washington Semillon

John Stuart Mill wrote: "That too few dare to be eccentric marks the chief danger of our time." Paul Thomas has that quote hanging on a wall in his winery, and it fits; if Blackwood Canyon's Mike Moore doesn't have it in his, he should. Mike is one of the most beloved characters in the business, and so are his often unusual wines. In recent years, he has done one thing consistently: he has made some of the most-flavorful, slightly off-dry, delightful Semillon in Washington. It's a wine deserving of a fine taste accompaniment such as this rich duck sausage.

MOLASSES RYE BREAD

I make these loaves very skinny so I get a small slice about 2 inches across to use as a base for appetizers or hors d'oeuves. They freeze quite well and are quite delicious with a little horseradish and pastrami!

½ c butter
2 oz unsweetened chocolate
2 Tb dry yeast
2 c strong coffee, warm
½ c molasses
½ c cider vinegar
5 c rye flour
1 Tb salt
2 Tb caraway seeds
1 tsp fennel seeds
5 c white flour
1 egg yolk

Melt the butter and chocolate.

Meanwhile, combine the yeast, warm coffee, molasses and vinegar in a large mixing bowl. Allow to sit while butter and chocolate cool. When the butter and chocolate are lukewarm, about 90°, add to the yeast mixture.

Beat in the rye flour, salt, caraway and fennel seeds with the dough hook attachment. Slowly add the white flour cup by cup until you have a soft dough.

Knead for 10 minutes, adding flour only as necessary to keep the dough from sticking to the bowl.

Place the dough in an oiled bowl and cover with a towel. Allow it to rise in a warm place until doubled in bulk, about 2 hours.

Divide the dough into 3 portions, cover and allow to rise for another 45 minutes.

Roll each portion into a rough rectangle and roll up into very skinny baguettes. Place each in a French bread pan and allow to rise for another 30 minutes.

continued...

Molasses Rye Bread

...continued

Brush with a mixture of 1 egg yolk and 1 tablespoon of water and bake in a preheated 350° oven for about 30 to 40 minutes. *Watch carefully to see that the tops don't overbrown. If they seem to be turning too brown, cover with foil.* Remove and cool on a bread rack.

This bread freezes quite well.

Makes 3 skinny baguettes.

When Pamela was testing this recipe for us, she refrigerated half of the dough overnight and made rolls for us all the next day—yummy.

ESCARGOTS

Bonair Winery Chateau Puryear Vineyard Chardonnay

Shirley Puryear is a crazy lady: She wears baseball caps to elegant wine dinners and pulls it off with aplomb. She and husband Gail can get away with quite a bit since they are *Bonair Winery, a lovely spot tucked away down a dirt road in the Zillah hills. And they make good wines, which they love to have people enjoy. This Chardonnay, made from estate-grown grapes, is one of their best. It's a wine strong enough for this classic escargot preparation.*

Ten years ago when we opened, our manager, Blaine Walker, was operating a fledgling snail farm and providing us with farm-raised snails. An unseasonably wet (even for the Peninsula) winter drowned the entire herd and forced him to re-organize as a cottage industry. Peninsula residents began collecting our local snails (the same variety as the French Burgundian snail) and bringing them to us. We use them all!

24 escargots, rinsed
2 c dry white wine
2 Tb brandy
pinch thyme
2 c butter
2 shallots, finely chopped
1 Tb garlic, minced
¼ c parsley, finely chopped
½ c Oregon hazelnuts, coarsely chopped

Marinate the escargots overnight in the white wine, brandy and thyme.

Heat 4 ceramic escargot ramekins for 5 minutes in a 500° oven. *As an alternative to the snail ramekins, use any single-serving sized casserole or souffle dish. Make sure it is heat-proof and that you heat it in the oven before adding the hot butter.*

Melt the butter in a large sauté pan and mix in the shallots, garlic, parsley and nuts.

Drain snails and add them to the butter mixture. Heat them over medium-high heat until just bubbling.

Distribute snails among the heated ramekins and pour the hot bubbling butter over them. Serve immediately with French bread.

Makes 4 servings.

Cranberry Champagne Soup

8 c cranberry juice
1 bottle champagne
3 c heavy cream
2 eggs
2 egg yolks
1/4 tsp cinnamon
1/4 tsp nutmeg
1/4 c brandy
juice of **1** lemon

Simmer cranberry juice and champagne until reduced by half.

In a mixer, beat 1 cup of the cream with eggs, egg yolks, cinnamon and nutmeg until frothy.

Slowly add egg mixture into the hot juices, whisking constantly. Simmer until the mixture thickens, stirring constantly.

Remove from heat, add brandy and the remaining 2 cups of cream and lemon juice. If serving the soup hot, bring it to a simmer and heat it through.

Serve hot or cold with a dash of nutmeg.

For a thicker, tangier soup, substitute the following purée for the cranberry juice: Simmer 12 cups cranberries in 8 cups of water with 3/4 cup sugar until the berries pop. Press through a sieve to equal 8 cups of purée.

Makes 8 servings.

Staton Hills Vineyards Washington Johannisberg Riesling

You know you're getting old when cops and winemakers start looking like kids to you. Rob Stuart only looks like a kid—underneath that facade, he is making a lot of serious, very good wine. Staton Hills is the first Washington winery to sell an interest to the Japanese, where they now market almost 40% of their production. Their Riesling is a nicely-balanced off dry fruity wine, a real Washington match with this soup made from our favorite local cranberries.

SIX-ONION SOUP

Portteus Vineyards Yakima Valley Chardonnay

Portteus Vineyards boasts the vineyard at the highest altitude in the state, located high on a plateau in the Zillah hills. Paul Portteus claims this directly results in very ripe, intensely-flavored grapes. He has been selling those grapes to major Washington wineries for years, but recently has ventured into his own label, making high-quality Chardonnay and Cabernet Sauvignon. This Chardonnay has the body to stand up to this rich onion soup.

½ c butter
1 large yellow onion, peeled & sliced
1 large red onion, peeled & sliced
1 bunch leeks, cleaned thoroughly & sliced, white part only
2 shallots, minced
4 cloves garlic, minced
1 oz chives, chopped fine
½ tsp kosher salt
1 tsp nutmeg
1 tsp thyme
½ tsp paprika
4 c heavy cream
4 c chicken stock
1½ tsp Worchestershire
CRISP-FRIED ONIONS

Melt the butter in a large sauce pan over medium-high heat and sauté the onions, leeks, shallots, garlic and chives until golden and soft.

Add the salt and spices and continue cooking for 5 more minutes, stirring gently to combine.

To freeze: Add the stock and Worchestershire but omit the cream; freeze before the final simmer. When you are ready to finish the soup, thaw the base, add the cream and bring it to a boil. Simmer 45 minutes and serve.

Add the cream, stock and Worchestershire. Bring to a boil, reduce the heat and simmer, uncovered, for 45 minutes.

Correct the seasonings, if necessary, and serve in warm bowls with garlic croutons or CRISP-FRIED ONIONS.

MAKES 8 CUPS.

SIX-ONION SOUP

CRISP-FRIED ONIONS

To make crisp-fried onions, heat 4 cups of peanut oil in a deep sauce pan to 360°. Slice 1 red onion very thin, separate the pieces, and drop into the oil in two batches. Deep-fry until golden brown then drain on paper towels. They will crisp up as they cool. I use these as a garnish with veal or beef dishes, also.

Chanterelle-Port Sturgeon

...continued

heated through. Deglaze with the vinegar and add the salt and pepper. Simmer until the liquid is almost all absorbed.

Add the cream to the 2 cups of reduced juice. Simmer until the sauce measures 2 cups. Add the mushrooms and vinegar reduction and reduce to 2 cups. Add the remaining 8 tablespoons of butter and simmer until it is reduced to 2 cups and it coats a spoon. Keep the sauce warm in a water bath while you grill the sturgeon.

Grill the sturgeon fillets about 5 minutes on the first side, turn them over and continue cooking until just firm to the touch, about 3 to 4 more minutes.

To serve, ladle ¼ cup of the sauce on each plate and set a fillet in the middle. Garnish with sprigs of fresh tarragon and a few cranberries.

Makes 8 servings.

The Shoalwater has always been a family affair. Of course, Tony and Ann and Blaine and Cheri, but lately Jenny, our older daughter has been working in the dining room. Our younger daughter Michelle became quite involved with the opening of our second restaurant The Lightship. And both Jenny and Michelle and Blaine and Cheri's daughter Bryn can be found around the office on their way to or from school, or riding, or ballet, or basketball.

Hazelnut & Cabernet Veal

Portteus Vineyards Yakima Valley Cabernet Sauvignon
To date, Paul Portteus has released three vintages of Cabernet Sauvignon, showing great promise with his ripe, intense wines to make even better examples in the future. Just a couple of years of aging of his first two releases have already proven that the wines are only improving and becoming more interesting as they spend more time at rest. A label definitely worth watching for. This wine coupled with Cheri's hazelnut and cabernet veal provides a taste worth waiting for.

1 bottle Cabernet

1 c veal demi-glace (**2 c** Shoalwater Veal Stock reduced to 1 c)

½ c hazelnuts, toasted & coarsely ground

1 c heavy cream

2 Tb butter, chilled & cut into bits

¼ tsp salt

½ tsp black pepper

2 lb veal medallions

additional ground hazelnuts, for garnish

Reduce the wine, demi-glace and hazelnuts over high heat to a thick syrupy glaze, about ½ cup. *Watch it carefully towards the end to avoid burning.*

Add the cream, whisking well. Bring to a slow boil and reduce to 1 cup, about 5 minutes.

Add the butter, a bit at a time, whisking continuously. Stir in the salt and pepper and hold the sauce over a hot water bath to keep warm while cooking the veal.

Sauté the veal medallions to desired degree of doneness.

Place a generous puddle of sauce on each plate and place the veal medallions on top. Garnish with hazelnuts.

Makes 4 servings.

Cranberry-Swirl Cheesecake

2 lb cream cheese, softened
1 $\frac{3}{4}$ c sugar
4 large eggs
2 c Cranberry Purée
4 oz Callebaut semisweet chocolate
$\frac{1}{4}$ c water
whipped cream & cranberries, for garnish

Blackwood Canyon
Ultra Late Harvest Riesling
And then, there is Mike Moore's Ultra Late Harvest Riesling... We match it with my favorite, Ann's prize-winning cheesecake.

Cream together the cream cheese and sugar, scraping the bowl well. *There should be no lumps.*

Add the eggs one at a time, scraping the bowl between additions.

Pour a third of the batter evenly into a buttered and lined 8 by 3 inch pan and drizzle 2 tablespoons of the Cranberry Purée over the top.

Pour another third of the batter over the purée, trying not to disturb the pattern, and then drizzle 2 more tablespoons of Cranberry Purée over the top. Pour in the remaining batter, smoothing carefully.

Place the cheesecake in a pan containing enough water to come halfway up the sides of the cheesecake pan. *If you are using a springform pan, be sure to wrap it in foil so the water from the water bath doesn't seep into the batter.* Bake in a preheated 350° oven until set in the center, about 1$\frac{1}{2}$-hours.

Cool completely, then turn out onto a serving platter and refrigerate. *The cheesecake freezes well at this point. To serve, thaw to refrigerated temperature before glazing.*

For the glaze, melt the chocolate and water in a microwave or over low heat.

continued...

CRANBERRY-SWIRL CHEESECAKE

...continued

This recipe won the 1988 Ocean Spray contest for the best cranberry dessert. The judges particularly liked the "New York style" lightness and the fact that the cake lends itself to easy decoration according to your mood. At Christmas, gather some holly and ring the top with leaves and fresh cranberries or simply garnish with whipped cream rosettes and candied cranberries.

Whisk in ¼ cup of the CRANBERRY PURÉE until the mixture is smooth and shiny. Allow to cool until thick enough to coat the cheesecake.

Pour the glaze over the cheesecake, creating a thick layer. Smooth the top with a flat knife, allowing large, even dribbles to decorate the sides of the cheesecake.

To serve, thin the remaining CRANBERRY PURÉE with a little water until you have a sauce. Pool some sauce on each plate and top with a piece of cheese-cake. Garnish with cranberries and lightly sweet-ened whipped cream rosettes. *Holly leaves make a nice garnish for the winter holiday season.* Send the remaining sauce around in a small pitcher.

Makes one 8-inch cheesecake.

Cranberry-Swirl Cheesecake

Cranberry Purée

4 c cranberries
1 c water
1 c sugar

Combine cranberries, water and sugar in a sauce pan and bring to a boil. Simmer until the berries pop, about 15 minutes.

Allow to cool, then purée in a food processer or blender. *You can strain the purée when it is hot, but be careful when you process it: hot liquids explode out of blenders.*

Strain out skins and seeds, then chill.

This sauce keeps well for up to 1 week, refrigerated.

Makes 2 cups.

Acknowledgements

The publication of our first book provides a perfect opportunity to recognize and acknowledge all those who have helped and supported us over the years and more recently in the writing of this book.

If we really got into it and began to name individually all those who have contributed to us and to our restaurant careers, this would be the longest chapter in the book. But no matter how many people we remembered to acknowledge, we would undoubtedly forget (and inadvertently upset) many important folks.

Therefore, with the few exceptions below, we offer a blanket thanks to all of you—family, friends, teachers, mentors, restaurateurs, winemakers, suppliers, business associates, staff members and customers—who have touched our lives and contributed to who we are and what we have achieved. We appreciate and love you all for all the help, encouragement, feedback, etc., you have given us.

We would like to acknowledge specifically:

–our daughters, Jenny and Michelle, and Blaine and Cheri's daughter Bryn, for being as great as they are and for their understanding of the crazy lives we lead in attempting to keep up with both a business and family life;

–our parents, without whose help none of us would even be here (in more ways than one); Adele and Ed Doolittle (Ann), Margaret and Simon Kischner (Tony), and Peggy and Dick Krusemark (Cheri);

–all our brothers, sisters and their families for constant extended family support;

–our manager (and Cheri's husband) Blaine Walker, for his hard work in furthering our vision for the restaurant and his unrelenting support of ourselves and Cheri;

–our close Seattle friends who supported and encouraged us in pursuing this crazy venture (and have remained true), even though it meant distance would separate us for the long term;

–Chef Dominique Place of Seattle, whose extraordinary (and seemingly effortless) cooking abilities have always been a source of awe and inspiration to us and whose basic teachings provided the catapult for Cheri's career when she first expressed an interest in cooking professionally;

–our newer friends on the Long Beach Peninsula, who have made this area an even greater place to live and have helped us immeasurably through the darkest winters;

–David Campiche and Laurie Anderson, Shelburne Inn owners, for their love, encouragement and very real support of our dream;

–Peggy and Eric Christiansen, of Long Beach's Grey Whale Gallery, for their loan of so many of the lovely dishes and utensils which appear in Joel Levin's beautiful photos in this book;

–Angela Harris and Dick Friedrich, our publishers, for getting this five-year-old "good idea" finally to happen, mostly by convincing us it really could be done.

Ann and Tony Kischner
Cheri Walker

CONTRIBUTORS

Tony Kischner grew up in Brazil, moving to the United States to attend Whitman College in Walla Walla, Washington. There he met New York born Ann Doolittle, who had been raised in Bellevue, Washington. They settled in Seattle where Tony managed Rosellini's Other Place. In 1981, they moved to Seaview, Washington, to operate a restaurant in the historic Shelburne Inn. To celebrate the Shoalwater's tenth anniversary the Kischners, with their chef Cheri Walker, have written *The Shoalwater's Finest Dinners*. Tony has provided commentary on the matching of food to wine as well as the story of the restaurant and their philosophy of food and wine.

Ann Kischner's desserts and breads have developed quite a following among regular diners at The Shoalwater. In this new cookbook, she shares some favorites such as her Bread Pudding. As well as baking and managing the restaurant business with her husband, Ann serves on the School Board of the Ocean Beach School District.

Cheri Walker, a classically trained musician (the harp), was a charter member of the Shoalwater staff, first co-managing with her husband Blaine and then training to move into the kitchen. She ultimately took over the position of chef and since then, using the Northwest's freshest and finest foods, has worked with the Kischners to develop the kind of dining experience that is the heart of their restaurant and of this book.

CONTRIBUTORS

Joel Levin, Seattle based photographer, has seen his work appear in books, newspapers and magazines around the country. He has captured in his photos the spirit and feel of a dinner at The Shoalwater. Another classically trained musician (trumpet), Levin was born in Chicago and has lived in Mexico, as well as Holland and Israel.

April Ryan designed and produced a dozen cookbooks before *The Shoalwater's Finest Dinners.* Born in Guadalajara, Mexico, she studied art and graphic design at the University of Washington and has recently moved competely to computer-based design and production.

INDEX

A

B

INDEX

C

INDEX

INDEX

D

E

F

INDEX

INDEX

I

J

K

L

M

INDEX

N

O

INDEX

INDEX

INDEX

INDEX

T

INDEX